D0655179

Shopping 3.0

Shopping 3.0

Buyers suddenly have a full overview of the range on offer, at all times

This freedom of choice gives buyers unlimited possibilities of buying anything and everything, wherever and however they want. Sellers have to adjust to this. Milton Friedman correctly stated that consumer demand steers with an invisible hand, so that the supply is modified to changes in demand (the demand paradigm).

Suppliers have to adapt to changes

Charles Darwin pointed out that flexibility is the basis of survival. In dynamic markets response to change must be rapid (the supply paradigm).

Integration of a different buying behaviour with a clearly defined and unlimited supply

A complete approach is especially necessary during changes in consumer behaviour due to technology (the Internet) and the economy (recession). What do customers want, what do customers do and what do customers buy? To be successful retailers and suppliers need to understand the customer and take advantage of the new style of shopping.

Suddenly all infrastructures combine

Telecommunications, mobile phones, Internet, cable, satellite and the physical all converge. We find ourselves on the eve of a major restructuring of how we live, work and shop!

Shopping 3.0

Shopping, the Internet or Both?

COR MOLENAAR

GOWER

Published by
Gower Publishing Limited
Wey Court East
Union Road
Farnham
Surrey, GU9 7PT
England

Ashgate Publishing Company
Suite 420
101 Cherry Street
Burlington,
VT 05401-4405
USA

www.gowerpublishing.com

British Library Cataloguing in Publication Data
Molenaar, Cor.
  Shopping 3.0 : shopping, the Internet or both?.
  1. Shopping. 2. Consumer behavior. 3. Marketing--
  Management. 4. Retail trade--Technological innovations.
  I. Title
  658.8-dc22

  ISBN: 978-1-4094-1764-4 (hbk)
      978-1-4094-1765-1 (ebk)

Library of Congress Cataloging-in-Publication Data
Molenaar, Cor.
  Shopping 3.0 : shopping, the Internet or both? / Cor Molenaar.
    p. cm.
  Includes index.
  ISBN 978-1-4094-1764-4 (hbk.) -- ISBN 978-1-4094-1765-1 (ebook)
  1. Electronic commerce. 2. Teleshopping. 3. Retail trade. 4. Consumer behavior.
  I. Title.
  HF5548.32.M65 2010
  658.8'72--dc22

                                                                          2010033175

Mixed Sources
Product group from well-managed
forests and other controlled sources
www.fsc.org Cert no. SA-COC-1565
© 1996 Forest Stewardship Council

Printed and bound in Great Britain by
MPG Books Group, UK

Contents

List of Figures   *vii*

List of Tables   *ix*

About the Author   *xi*

Introduction: Retailers in Difficult Times   1

1   8pm in the Evening: How Life has Changed for Retailers   9

2   A New Way of Shopping: The Role of Customer Experience
     and Entertainment   45

3   Shopping Evolution: How to Adapt to Survive   71

4   Customers Want Recognition: Making the Shopping
     Experience Personal   105

5   Technology Makes Buying Easy: Integrating Bricks and
     Mortar with the Internet   139

6   The Future of Shopping: Shopping, the Internet or Both?   173

Appendix 1: The Competing Values Model   *199*

Appendix 2   *201*

Index   *203*

List of Figures

Figure I.1   Shops will adapt to the new Shopping 3.0   5
Figure 1.1   The ORCA buying model: Orientation, Research,
               Communication/Contemplating, Action   14
Figure 1.2   Influences on relationships between customers (buying
               reasons) and shops (location, assortment, services and
               external influences)   18
Figure 1.3   The supply-driven paradigm   26
Figure 1.4   Suppliers sell direct to customers by using their own shops
               or the Internet   29
Figure 1.5   People who made electronic purchases in the last 12
               months   38
Figure 2.1   The Shopping 3.0 model   56
Figure 4.1   Evolutionary impact of the Internet on retailing   107
Figure 4.2   Phase 1, digitization of the buying processing and
               information   118
Figure 4.3   Phase 2, digitization of products, made downloadable   119
Figure 4.4   Phase 3, specific digital devices become available   119
Figure 4.5   The pre- and post-Internet retail landscape   124
Figure 4.6   A combination of virtual reality and physical shopping   135
Figure 5.1   The shift from distributor to customer service point   147
Figure 5.2   Generating buying suggestions based on customer profiles   153
Figure 5.3   Information process for customers   161
Figure 5.4   Single source of data for product information   164
Figure 5.5   Solution overview   164
Figure 5.6   The software solution   169
Figure 6.1   Intelligent home portals   186
Figure A.1   The Competing Values model   199

List of Tables

Table 1.1   Growth in number of shops broken down by branch and
             shopping area 2003–2007 (in %)   12
Table 1.2   Digital natives and digital immigrants   15
Table 1.3   Growth in online sales in Europe   31
Table 1.4   Most popular websites in the UK in 2009   35
Table 1.5   Household access to the Internet in 2008   37
Table 1.6   The difference between physical buying and buying on the
             Internet   40
Table 1.7   Advantages and disadvantages of physical shopping versus
             web shopping   41
Table 2.1   Customer satisfaction scores for the top UK pure-play online
             retailers, December 2009   47
Table 2.2   Differences between the classic buying process and new-style
             shopping   59
Table 3.1   Exogenous and endogenous factors influencing an
             organization   78
Table 3.2   Historical development of retail and technology   92
Table 4.1   Browser statistics month by month (%)   133
Table 5.1   Use of the Internet and information technology   165
Table 6.1   Buying preferences based on types of articles   178

About the Author

Professor Dr. C.N.A. (Cor) Molenaar is an authority in the field of marketing and the Internet. As a visionary and trend watcher he has a clear vision of future developments, based on continuous scientific research. He is an Associate Professor at the Rotterdam School of Management of the Erasmus University in Rotterdam. His chair in eMarketing & Distance Selling covers research into the impact of technology on marketing, and the developments of e-commerce and the Internet in sales. He also teaches the topic eMarketing & Distance Selling as part of the regular Master's course.[1]

Professor Molenaar is also Chairman of the RFID Platform Nederland, a platform for contactless registration on the basis of the Radio Frequency Identification (RFID) chip, and Chairman of the Foundation for Homeshopping Security.

He is frequently invited to speak at conferences and at in-house company events in Europe and further afield. In addition, he acts as advisor and/or commissioner to various leading companies and is Director of the strategic consultancy eXQuo Consultancy in Oosterbeek.

Professor Molenaar has written several books, some of which have also been published in Spanish, Italian, English and even Chinese. These books include: *The Future of Marketing* (2000), *Interactive Marketing* (1995), *Surviving the Internet* (2007) and *eMarketing* (2010).

He writes a monthly e-newsletter and has his own website: www.cormolenaar.nl.

---

1   The chair in eMarketing & Distance Selling is sponsored by leading companies that include Cap Gemini, DHL, GFK Technology and Retail, hybris software and the Homeshopping society (thuiswinkel.org). On behalf of Thuiswinkel.org the following 8 companies are sub-sponsors: BOL.com, Wehkamp, Neckerman, Otto, Conrad, ECI, Sundio/Sunweb, Achmea.

Shopping 1.0

Buying from local shops or craftsmen. Sometimes 'off the shelf', sometimes handmade.

Shopping 2.0

Non-store retailing. Mail order companies, door-to-door sales, coupons form an alternative to local shops and craftsmen.
Practically only 'ready made' products are sold.

Shopping 3.0

Buyers are using all channels for information and shopping. Mostly information is first gathered from the Internet before checking in the store.
A decision is made to buy online or in the store (cross-channel retailing based on buying behaviour).

(v) hybris software
THE AGILE RESPONSE

ARE YOU READY FOR CROSS-CHANNEL COMMERCE?

As retailers consider adding yet another channel to the sales and marketing mix, consistency of product information becomes increasingly critical.

Retailers have been talking about cross-channel retailing for many years. At first, consumers had a choice between making their purchases in store and catalogue shopping. But when the Internet arrived, retailing was revolutionized beyond recognition, offering the potential to reach far greater numbers of consumers with a much more flexible and immediate service. The introduction of mobile commerce looks set to turn everything on its head once again, but how many businesses that talk about cross-channel retailing are really ready for it?

Inconsistency of product information across different channels is a big issue that continues to trouble retailers. It will only be exacerbated with the addition of mobile commerce as consumers are offered the chance to compare prices and products via their mobile handsets "on the go," review "edited choice" lists based on recent purchasing history, make purchases via online catalogues, scan product barcodes in store for possible purchase at a later date, and request pickup, delivery, and returns from any location.

With the consumer calling all the shots, it will only take one bad experience – whether it be out-of-date pricing, incorrect information about sizing, color, or availability, or the inability to offer a tailored and personalized shopping experience – for that consumer to switch brands or change their retail outlet to make their purchase.

The mobile and Internet channels are capable of changing and responding quickly to meet the individual needs of consumers, but retailers must be able to identify individual customers when they log in to a site and then present them with an experience tailored to their needs. Both channels are able to carry and promote an extensive range, but if product search, "if you liked this, you'll love this" comparison, and speed of purchase are not managed well and presented to the consumer in an easy-to-use manner, sales will be lost.

At the heart of the successful inclusion of the mobile channel into any cross-channel retailing strategy is data integrity. The integration and consistency of product information across all channels must be assured if reputation-damaging data error is to be eliminated.

Centralizing all product data in one location on a product information management (PIM) platform will enable retailers to create a single source of product data that is fed to all channels simultaneously.

This should be the starting point for real integration across the business and an end to the empire building that typifies the departmental structure of many retailers. Integration of data and business processes behind the scenes should enable retailers to take advantage of the new cross-channel world that customers increasingly favor. It should help retailers operate as a single business with one cost center fighting to win and retain customers, not separate channels with different revenue streams, fighting against each other to be the lead channel.

As competition between retailers becomes more fierce, the key will be delivering the right product and services, at the right price, to the right customer, at the right time. Consumers will increasingly become channel agnostic. Internal battles over which channel is the flagship store or reporting the highest sales is irrelevant. The consumer only sees the brand, not the delivery mechanism.

The technology is there to make cross-channel retailing a reality, but if the walls between departments are not broken down, if the systems supporting each channel are not integrated, if information about products, services, and promotions is not consistent, if the customer is not placed at the center of all communications, customers will go elsewhere.

Hybris is happy to provide to you with this insightful book covering the complexities and opportunities in cross-channel retailing. For more details about how hybris can help you please visit: www.hybris.com

Introduction:
Retailers in Difficult Times

A few years from now, when the banks are wholly owned by the government, our houses are worth less than our cars and we have to travel by rickshaw, we'll be telling our grandchildren about the days when we used to go to 'shops' to buy clothes. How will we explain the phenomenon of whole buildings being used not to house thousands of redundant bankers and estate agents but to store rail after rail of clothes?

Too futuristic? Perhaps. But if the shop isn't quite dead, 2009 will certainly be remembered as the year when it started losing its fight against the internet. IMRG, the online retail industry body, reported a 34 per cent increase in online shopping last year. Industry insiders are predicting that by 2016 the online fashion business will account for 13 per cent of the fashion market and be worth some £6 billion.

Source: *Daily Telegraph*, 3 February 2009.

Retailers are enduring difficult times. The recession, government regulation and the rise of the Internet all mean that costs and competition are rising but turnover is not.

The high streets are the same across the whole country; the same shops wherever you go. Customers are increasingly deserting the high street shops because there is an alternative: the Internet. However, that is not the only issue. Customers have become much choosier; they will no longer allow themselves to be categorized and they are critical about price, service and the products themselves.

Customers have also busier lifestyle nowadays, and they are making different shopping choices. In simple terms, singles have a strong need for social contact, the elderly want to stay in their own neighbourhood, people aged between 30 and 45 are occupied with their children, their relationship, their job, moneymaking and, of course, with themselves. They have plenty of ambition but little time.

And the retailer? The retailer simply waits in his or her shop until the customers come. The retailer clings to old habits: fixed price, fixed opening hours, often an unchanging layout in the shop and newspaper or leaflet advertising only. Changes in consumer buying behaviour have not stimulated a change in the 'real' shop retail approach, the reasons customers purchase what they do has not been addressed and the only time technology is utilized is during the payment process at the cash desk. Retailers are, as it were, transaction driven and not customer driven. To create real change, retailers should focus on the relationship with customers rather than on just making a transaction.

The Internet

Business is no longer about selling but about buying; we don't talk of sales processes but about buying processes. Customers don't come into a shop because they have to; they enter a shop voluntarily because it is attractive to them or serves a purpose. Shops are far from being written off but they have considerable work to do. Retailers must think about customers' purchasing behaviour and their reasons for buying through each medium. Why is the Internet a success? What place will the Internet occupy in the purchasing process? Is it practical for customers to buy through the Internet? Internet selling is actually not as easy as retailers may think: customers have to know and trust the site, pay in advance and then await delivery of their purchases (which can take at least one day and very often longer). When placing orders with overseas retailers there is also the concern of whether it will arrive at all. Each channel has its pros and cons.

The Internet is a medium in which the customer can be the central focus. Internet retailers know more about their customers than could ever be possible in a 'real' shop. The integrated application of technology enables Internet retailers to track users' activities, such as navigation and buying behaviours. If a user enters a login code, or places an order, then the picture is complete. The name, address, personal details, IP address and the visiting and purchasing behaviour can be carefully recorded in a database. Customer profiles can be created and communications can be personally tailored and directed, at minimal cost, either through the Internet or, less often, by regular mail. This is a dream world for the large professional Internet suppliers, but there are also disadvantages:

- How can you attract customers to your site?

- How can you encourage customers to buy when you can't see them?

- Do customers actually read all those e-mails (on average only 17 per cent do)?

Additionally, web retailers may not have sufficient knowledge about the possibilities offered by the technology they have available to them and the investment in a professional e-commerce environment is costly and time-limited. An average Internet site has to be revamped every three years. Technology changes, fashion changes, but it's the customers who undergo the greatest change.

The Shop

This book examines all of these customer changes. It sketches the world of consumers; both those who make their purchases from the comfort of their armchair and those who enjoy shopping as a social experience. This book outlines the problems facing the retailer and also the possibilities, opportunities and challenges, because, even in shrinking markets, there will always be winners.

The magazine *The Architect* took a detailed look at shopping 3.0 and what this means for architecture and the layout of a shop:

> *The criteria set for a shop interior are considerably higher than ten years ago. Where previously the interior was presumed to be restrained, nowadays the idea is that the design of the space and the product enhance each other. This is the consequence of the new shopping culture. Now that almost anything can be bought on the Internet, shops should have an added value and evoke an emotional reaction or experience. Consumers want to experience something, have a bite to eat, meet friends, learn something and, above all, be aware of it. Simultaneously the commissioning party's customers want their brand values to be*

strongly communicated. That demands a re-evaluation of shop design
and a new approach by designers and architects.

Source: *The Architect*, 22 March 2007.

Shops will fulfil a new role: a social role, a role as a social meeting place, a 'feel at home' role. Authenticity will also be important: giving a sense of being different, being genuine and 'suiting me'. A price war will break out between Internet suppliers and real shops on the basis of ratio. In some cases this is already happening with 'lowest price guarantees' and 'guaranteed the cheapest'. Customer buying is not only based on price alone, it is also based on personal motives.

Mass shopping is not something that has always been around; shops only became concentrated in town centres at the start of the twentieth century. The 'fun' element of shopping became more evident in relation to increased leisure time and mobility in the 1960s and 1970s. Shopping became a way to pass the time. The local grocery shop disappeared from the high street in favour of out-of-town supermarkets with their own parking facilities. This changed the face of town centres as well, with the appearance of more shops selling the expensive, luxurious items not catered for by supermarkets. Town centres became places to browse and window shop and out-of-town shopping centres became a practical destination.

Now a new development is taking place which emphasizes the social character of a town centre as well as the process of shopping: convivial, fun and relaxing shopping is the watchword. This development will continue in the coming years, even after the recession. The focus of the town centre will be geared more towards entertainment with a shopping function (see Figure I.1). In addition, there will be an increasing number of out-of-town shopping centres featuring cinemas, sports centres and restaurants. The development of both town centres and out-of-town shopping centres into destinations featuring entertainment venues as well as shops are taking place in parallel, and the same is happening elsewhere in Europe. The focus of town centres will be on 'shopping goods' and luxurious items, and the out-of-town shopping centres will provide convenience. Theatres and exclusive restaurants are more likely to be located in town centres. New shops will also continue to appear in the old town centres, in villages and in the suburbs. Some of these may be a franchise of the major chains. These will be small shops offering a limited assortment meeting people's daily needs as well as 'click and collect' facilities for consumers ordering online and collecting instore.

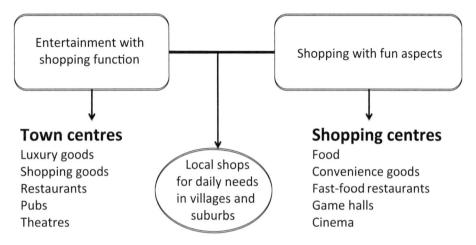

| Entertainment with shopping function | | Shopping with fun aspects |

Town centres
Luxury goods
Shopping goods
Restaurants
Pubs
Theatres

Local shops for daily needs in villages and suburbs

Shopping centres
Food
Convenience goods
Fast-food restaurants
Game halls
Cinema

Figure I.1   Shops will adapt to the new Shopping 3.0

> *Shops are changing into places that adopt more and more hospitality functions, like a café and this has consequences for the total concept and where the quality of the interior design is more important than ever. After all, a pleasant shop heightens the (emotional) values of the product bought there, so that the shop interior gradually becomes part of the range.*

Source: *The Architect*, 22 March 2007.

Society is also changing; technology is playing an increasingly important role in our lives. The changes as a result of major new infrastructures of the 1990s have not yet been realised. The renovation of the old infrastructures (such as motorways, radio and television) are in full swing, but these are often only modifications. In the meantime, the recession has forced companies to make changes to their organization and business model. It also resulted in a change in consumer buying behaviour. New shopping habits are only one aspect of this change in behaviour – new styles of working and living are arising from the integration of technology into our lives' work. This will be discussed in the final chapter. This change of behaviour, stimulated by the integration of technology, is the basis for the future, for our behaviour and for shopping. The technological infrastructures will show a strong convergence in the next decade, resulting in many of them merging. Users will be able to determine for themselves which medium suits them best: watching television on their mobile phone (mobile infrastructure), at home on their PC (Internet) via cable or perhaps via an antenna or a satellite. This applies to watching television, but also to telephoning or even shopping. These are challenging times. From an economic perspective, who will survive? How will society be changed by economic, social and international developments? Which technologies will be used and for what? However, people remain people, wherever they are only our behaviour changes. That is the message of this book.

MATCH THE DÉCOR TO YOUR CUSTOMERS' WISHES AND THE FUTURE WILL BE YOURS

The original idea for this book came to me during a boat trip around the Galapagos Islands, the region where Darwin found the basis for his theory of evolution. 'Adapt to survive' and 'It is not the strongest of the species that survive, but one most responsive to change' are two famous quotes from his book *The Origin of Species*. However, what applies to the animal and plant kingdoms may naturally also apply to people and organizations. The Internet is driving changes; who is going to be most responsive? This book is intended as a helping hand for retailers, bricks and mortar shopkeepers and web-shop retailers, to help you determine what you need to do.

The book is based on the customer who makes his purchases in large and small shops, locally or internationally. The customer determines what happens; the retailer chooses his own route. I would like to thank all colleagues, and those who attended my lectures and workshops, for the discussions and expansion of my vision. My thanks also go to my customers and colleagues at the RSM and, of course, also to my students. Naturally, once again, my wife Patricia has acted as my discussion partner and patiently waited until the book was ready before going on holiday. We didn't quite manage that, but I was able to finish it during the holiday. The sun that was shining then is shining now for all retailers who are flexible and can adapt to the 'shopping 3.0' of the modern customer.

In 2015 the retailing landscape will have transformed completely. Although a lot of the technologies around at the moment will be key to driving this change, they will have evolved considerably. For shoppers, the look and feel of shopping will continue to change as many existing retail concepts meet the end of their shelf life. Retail businesses will have to innovate continuously as an increasingly digital environment gives shoppers dramatic new choices. Consumer products manufacturers will need to respond to these trends and embrace new assumptions. These changes reflect many trends. The Baby Boom generation—which has dominated retail thinking for decades—will be turning 70 and the baton will be passed to Generation Y. Technology will become increasingly available. Shoppers will interact with retailers and suppliers more than ever before, with online capabilities and communities playing a bigger and bigger role in the relationship. The new future is unfolding now; this report provides a glimpse of what's in store for shoppers, for retailers, and for the manufacturers who create the myriad of consumer products we buy every day.

Source: www.TNSglobal.com, May 2008.

1

8pm in the Evening: How Life has Changed for Retailers

At 8pm in the evening, once the children are in bed, online retailers experience a surge in shopping activity. Laptops are opened and serious shopping begins: women's clothes, children's clothes, holidays. A rainy Sunday afternoon is no different. These are the moments when efficiency and the wish to buy converge. Being at home feeling cosy and relaxed is important but so too is the convenience of buying now. In the current financial climate, making purchases efficiently and pleasurably from the comfort of their own home is important to the consumer. Shopping is linked to moments: convenient moments, efficient moments, but also moments when you just want to buy. This can vary considerably by person; the traditional predictability of buying behaviour has become a thing of the past. Buying has become a personal experience, a personal choice with personal motivation. There is plenty of choice, from online to physical shopping, from home delivery to takeaway, from sensible shopping to leisure shopping with a Starbucks close by.

In sharp contrast to this is the overbearing attitude of national shop trading hours, which seem to be based on making shopping a privilege, protecting the entrepreneur and the private lives of a few.

Where is the reason in forcing shops to close when emotional obstacles to buying are at their lowest and when you fancy going shopping (in the evenings, at the weekend and especially on Sundays)? The streets are packed with people on Sundays when the shops are open. This is part of modern life. However, these signals are apparently not enough to allow the shops to open, for the benefit of their customers, whenever they want. Trading hours must be regulated, which means shops are closed when the legislator wants them to be, despite protests from retailers and consumers alike. This unintentionally encourages online shopping; there's no stopping the will and urge to buy so alternatives will be sought and indeed found. The impact this will have on retailers, shopping centres and town centres is conveniently overlooked. The Internet shops are open 24/7 and shopping online is becoming increasingly normal and trusted. This is naturally at the expense of local shops, more and more of which are being forced to close. Town centres and high streets are consequently losing their appeal. Customers and retailers have no choice; the market has changed but the legislator refuses to follow suit. And there are other developments that don't make the life of a retailer any easier!

ARE THE DAYS OF FUNSHOPPING OVER?

Visions of funshopping vary, which certainly does not create the impression that figures are dropping by tens of percent. Obviously some figures are rising, while others fall. Centres that are new and innovative are doing better, often at the expense of the older areas. In addition, in some inner cities there are other, sometimes regenerated town centres within the catchment area. There is a difference between large town centres (which often continue to do well) and smaller centres (where problems can sometimes occur). Generally speaking, however, there is no decline in the numbers of visitors.

Research currently being conducted by Q&A (at the behest of the Dutch Council of Shopping Centres) has revealed that 38 per cent of Dutch consumers describe themselves as a 'fun shopper', a percentage that has hardly changed in recent years. For women this is actually more than half. The same research also reveals that the most important reason for Dutch consumers to shop in a town centre (besides the proximity) is the atmosphere and social aspect. This is not much different from international reports from England and Germany. In big cities shopping became funshopping and entertainment like restaurants or a coffee shop are just as important as nice attractive shops.

Source: Dutch Shopping Centres Council [Nederlands Raad van Winkelcentra], 30 March 2009.

Life's Not Easy for Retailers!

Real shopping is actually an activity which fits perfectly into everyday life. Being physically active, allowing yourself to be led and tempted generates a sense of happiness for all shoppers, and some get even addicted to the thrill of shopping – as social creatures we all get a pleasurable feeling from buying something nice. We are delighted with our purchases and want to show them off straightaway, to anyone willing to see them! Desire and satisfaction coincide, as it were.

Is this still the case? The fun in real shopping is restricted in many ways. The weather is often an obstacle, but malls were invented to overcome that with multi-storey car parks and good connections with public transport, In old town centres, the traditional shopping centres where the well-to-do retailers ran their businesses, shopping is almost discouraged. Highly restrictive parking policies make it practically impossible and expensive to park anywhere near town centres, the conditions under which retailers can run a pavement café are restrictive (in terms of size, business hours and season), and altering the premises to make shopping more enjoyable is fine, provided the local council approves! If you then take various local taxes which push the costs even higher – from local tax to environmental taxes and levies – and add that to government policy on trading hours, the retailers are rightly very worried. Life's not easy for real retailers, customers are beginning to avoid town centres for those reasons and funshopping will go out of fashion unless the centres adapt to the new customers. Is there still any hope for real shopping?

> *Even before the recession, some High Streets were ailing as shopping habits shifted. High class regional shopping destinations, the move to 'leisure shopping', more demanding shoppers and the growing importance of the internet all pose significant challenges to traditional High Streets. But it's not all doom and gloom. Some High Streets have found ways to buck the trend.*
>
> *There is a bright future for High Streets as the focal point for local communities. Retailing will be an essential part of this future but is likely to have a changing role.*

Source: British Retail Consortium, July 2009.

The selection of shops available hasn't exactly contributed to enjoyable shopping experiences. Walk down any high street and you'll find the same variety of shops, anywhere in the country (see Table 1.1). The chain stores and franchise chains have turned shopping into a rational process, often with no smells, no colours and no surprises, everything is predictable. The small retailers, who gave a certain charm to shopping, have disappeared, taken over by chains, pushed out of existence by local policy, or having folded under the heavy cost of existence or due to the lack of a successor. The mixture of shops, including the quaint little shops that stocked everything but the kitchen sink, the nostalgia and the boutiques, has consequently disappeared out of view of the shopping public. So monotony and predictability rule in today's high streets and shops.

Table 1.1   Growth in number of shops broken down by branch and shopping area 2003–2007 (in %)

BRANCH	INNER CITIES	VILLAGE CENTRES +4%	SUBURBAN CENTRES	OTHERS
Secondhand items	-7%	+4	-10	-7%
Clothing	+3%	+9%	+3%	+5%
Literature	+2%	+8%	0%	-3%
Films/music/software	-9%	-22%	-9%	-33%
Travel	-17%	0%	+11%	-18%
Hardware	+25%	+27%	+41%	+12%
Photo/film	-33%	-25%	-30%	-33%
Brown and white goods	-30%	-13%	-24%	-17%
Other branches	+2%	+3%	+0%	+1%
Empty shops	-0%	+7%	-11%	-14%

Adapted from the figures for the Netherlands from Locatus (2003–2007) produced by Ruimtelijk Planbureau (2007).

Customers are Buying Differently

Customers have also changed. The little village shop, where shopkeepers knew their customers so well, has disappeared. Today's shops are attractive but very efficient, the retailer has staff who are often young and inexperienced, and who no longer know the names and preferences of the customers. It's often only a (part-time) job, and they're only doing it for the money. Of course the staff are only too pleased to advise the customer on their purchase, but that's as far as it goes. However, customers often want more than impersonal advice or a checkout transaction.

> *During a recent visit to Nepal I was surprised when a small shopkeeper told me how happy he was that I visited his shop, where another shopkeeper said to me: 'Thank you for spending your money in my shop.' It gave me a warm welcome and happy feeling.*

If you buy something online, you not only find lots of product information but also customer recognition. Past purchasing behaviour is recorded, as is all manner of personal and relevant information. This gives the customers the feeling that they have been recognized and that they are welcome. These traditional values, so characteristic of the 'corner shop', have become practically extinct in modern-day shopping, but customers still appreciate them nonetheless. This is one of the reasons that more and more small shops are again opening in the suburbs and small town centres: service is their weapon. Customers have also grown accustomed to the transparency the Internet provides and the ability to compare. People used to acquire that knowledge while shopping, trailing around shop after shop on a Saturday, in search of advice and material for comparison. Then, over a coffee or back at home, they would quietly evaluate the various possibilities and, without further ado, decide 'where to buy what'. The customer would then return to the shop to seal the deal. It might sound old-fashioned but it was both fun and effective. There you sat, the two of you, in a cosy café or at the kitchen table browsing through brochures and comparing, and then deciding on the purchase together.

Nowadays consumers get their information from the Internet, no longer trailing around the shops, but shopping from the comfort of their own home, in front of the TV, with their laptop on their knee. The customer then takes the information (product knowledge), customer experiences and prices with them to the shop and starts asking the staff very pertinent questions. Extensive Googling or Yahooing has already generated a host of information on a particular item the customer plans to buy and now there are a few specific questions the staff will be required to answer. Not an easy task for the sales assistant in a shop, of course. Today's consumers are also very price conscious, aware of the prices in well-known stores and web-shops, and even the prices abroad (through the Internet). Every purchase is really only one click away, and that is what retailers have to compete with: online suppliers anywhere in the country, or indeed anywhere in the world in some cases. Customers now consider haggling over the shop price a normal part of the buying process, with all its consequences for the retailer's margin.

> *The BCSC indicate that whilst online retailing will exert pressure on retail rental growth over the next five to ten years, this will be felt most acutely in smaller centres. Larger shopping centres will remain desirable destinations in which to shop, and are deemed virtually immune to the impact of online shopping. Physical stores will remain the most popular point of sale for retailers and expansions are set to continue, although greater use of websites will be made as a means of distributing goods to customers.*

Source: www.wigan.gov.uk.

A typical buying behaviour is shown in the ORCA model (Figure 1.1). How do we buy – from searching for information, to contemplating where and what to buy, examining the items, then buying in the shop or back home on the Internet? The customer has more choices – shopping 3.0 – than ever before.

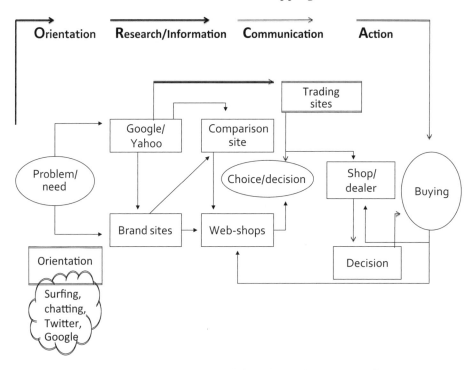

Figure 1.1   The ORCA buying model: Orientation, Research, Communication/Contemplating, Action

Immigrants versus Natives

Since the beginning of humanity, mankind has been surrounded by constant changes and transformations. Facing those frequent modifications, the human has had no other choice than to modify his habits in order to adopt the changes and live with them. The Internet is an excellent example of a change that humans have had to deal with. When the Internet appeared in our lives, a new era began. People learned how to work with this new revolutionary tool and accepted that computers and the Internet were now part of their daily routines. For those who experienced the emergence of the Internet later in life, this has meant adapting to the new possibilities. These people will stay immigrants and will always have a different behaviour to the youngster who never knew a life without the Internet.

For the younger generation the Internet is nothing special, just another useful tool among many others. Why aren't they amazed by the digital technologies like computers, the Internet or mobile phones? The reason is simple: those digital technologies were used before they were even born!

The latter represents a new generation often designated as 'Digital Natives'. Given the fact that they were born in a digital environment, the digital natives' lifestyle has nothing to do with their parents' way of living. They breathe through those digital tools. No need for an instruction booklet, they know in an inherent way how to use everything technological. Generally, natives are younger than 35 and digital immigrants are older than 35 (see Table 1.2).

Table 1.2   Digital natives and digital immigrants

Digital natives	Digital immigrants
Online is the same as offline. They feel connected and friendship like in real life.	Online is different to offline. They use the Internet for very specific personal reasons. The Internet is an add-on to real life.
They are always online, very sociable, well informed.	Online is a choice with a reason. It should fit in with their normal behaviour.
Early adopters, will try anything, strong group behaviour, use chatting, social media, mobile as fact of life.	Use e-mail, search for information and use the Internet for practical reasons.
Digital and physical are combined, they feel no difference.	Two separate worlds. The Internet is still a strange thing, no idea how it really works. It should fit in with my life.

Retailers are Struggling

All these developments are putting considerable pressure on retailers. With fewer customers, smaller margins, stricter regulations, competition from the Internet and competition from suppliers all over the world, it's no wonder that retailers are struggling! However, not every purchase is the same and not every sector faces the same problems. The various retailers and sectors can probably learn from each other. After all, according to Darwin, survival is also a matter of adapting to ever-changing circumstances. Flexibility is perhaps a key element of success; but what is particularly important to success is knowing the customers. What do customers buy and why do customers want to buy from me? In the traditional pattern, retailers are very supply oriented; product range, location and contacts are their core values. But today these values are under pressure. Why? Because customers are more mobile, because of the Internet and because of the different, often individual lifestyles we, the consumers, currently lead – with double incomes, working mothers and internationally oriented customers. Once again retailers must reconsider these core concepts, but this must be in the context of the buying behaviour and purchase requirements of (potential) customers. It certainly is an interesting challenge!

> *In terms of the comparison sector as a whole a concentration of national multiples into larger centres has occurred in recent times. As this takes place, the comparison retailing element of smaller centres has declined, with their role becoming principally a destination for convenience goods. Retail parks continue to be popular with comparison goods retailers, as these facilities allow large purpose built units to be obtained and often planning permissions permit the sale of a more diverse range of goods. Another effect of comparison traders increasingly seeking larger, more modern premises has been a trend for national multiples to favour covered, purpose built shopping malls within town centres, such as the new Grand Arcades development in Wigan. As a result the focus of retailing within town centres has shifted from the high street to managed shopping centres.*

Source: www.Wigan.gov.uk.

Shopping can also be Fun

There are two important patterns very obvious in the buying behaviour of consumers: the rational behaviour and the emotional behaviour. Rational behaviour belongs to rational shoppers: buying and shopping out of necessity, driven by price or convenience. For emotional shoppers it is much more about the experience. Shopping is enjoyable, it is fun. Whether anything is actually bought is of minor importance. Shopping is a hobby, an enjoyable pastime. Sometimes you do it alone, but often with friends or family.

There's also a distinction in what you buy. Are these products you don't have to think about, often necessities such as groceries, or are they products that you do need to think about before you go shopping? This is a distinction in terms of convenience goods and items for which you shop (shopping goods). There's another distinct category that needs more time and attention, which we can label luxury products. These can vary from cars and houses to exclusive watches; a special category, therefore, to which very special buying rules apply.

> *The Web is shaping up to be one of retail's bright spots this holiday season, thanks in part to a new take on an old-fashioned retail idea: good service.*

> *At a time when traditional retailers are being ultra conservative, many Web sites have been spending to make shipping times faster, consumer-generated reviews better, and to offer new features such as online layaways. Amazon.com Inc. is rolling out more 'frustration-free' packages that replace hard-to-open plastic clamshells; eBay Inc. is highlighting merchants with the best ratings; and Sears Holdings Corp. is launching online layaway.*

Source: *Wall Street Journal*, 28 October 2009.

Changes are seen in all the above categories, but changes are also visible in buying behaviour and in the range of goods on offer. Supermarkets try to aim their range of goods and concept more and more at specific target groups; brand manufacturers are having to battle against all the own brand goods, with the battle being fought on the supermarket shelves. Manufacturers and retailers are competing for customers and also considering the opportunities created by the Internet. The result is a complex series of changes and adaptations, on the part of both the customer and the supplier (see Figure 1.2).

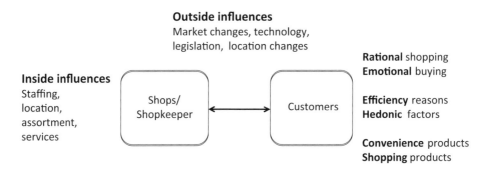

Figure 1.2   Influences on relationships between customers (buying reasons) and shops (location, assortment, services and external influences)

Entrepreneurs Have a Challenge

SHOPPING 3.0

Challenges are interesting and bring a bit of colour to everyday life, but challenges must also be attainable. The challenges currently faced by retailers are bigger than ever. The scale of the competition has increased with the arrival of chain stores and franchises, and the competitive market has become nationwide and sometimes worldwide through the Internet. In addition, the economic circumstances (the credit crisis followed by the recession) are not positive, affecting employment, purchasing power and consumer confidence. The Internet has introduced a new way of shopping which has lots of advantages and is developing strongly: items are increasingly bought online and age restrictions no longer really exist. People wishing to spend the winter months in Spain can book their plane ticket and rental car on the Internet, sitting on the couch at home with their laptop on their knee, a cosy fire burning and a glass of wine and their partner close by. What a happy situation in which to make a purchase; let's drink to a successful holiday or a successful purchase!

The Internet has made it easy to compare prices and information on all sorts of goods. Making the purchase is simple and goods are delivered directly to your door. This leads to *two* joyous moments for the customers, the moment of purchase and the moment of delivery to their home. Sometimes the products are 'downloadable', such as music, software or e-books. As for the purchase of services, nothing else needs to be done: you can book plane tickets and fly without a physical ticket. Life has thus become extremely easy for consumers, but this also poses a direct threat to existing retailers. Facing so many challenges and so many changes, the traditional shopkeeper is disappearing, leaving behind empty shopping streets, shopping centres with an identical range of shops and products, and making small independent shops almost a dying trade. The consumer makes the choice on where to shop and – with the help of the government – holds the destiny of the shopkeeper. The misery does not appear to end there, however...

Brands

Brands are important for the relationship between manufacturers and customers. A brand leads to recognition and a positive association, generated through carefully controlled advertising campaigns. Brands have always had the benefit of trust. They are generally known and widely available at a constant price, with constant quality, constant quantity and identical packaging. They are recognizable and customers have confidence in them. Many brand commercials are so evocative that they create a positive brand experience.

Brands became increasingly important in the 1950s. Consumers had more money to spend, welfare improved immensely, advertisements became more professional, and there was also a breakthrough of mass media, such as radio, television and, to a certain extent, newspapers and magazines. These developments reinforced each other but at the same time it became increasingly difficult for consumers to make a choice from the large range of items on offer; mass production led to mass supply. Shops increasingly turned to self-service, so that customers had to make a choice themselves without the direct help of the shopkeeper or shop assistants. This was the decade of an increasing number of shops, more and more chain stores found themselves sharing major shopping streets in town centres and cities. In this confusing situation, in which there were many simultaneous or consecutive developments, two buying patterns could be discerned: a routine purchase, whereby personal experiences led to repeated purchases, and recognizability, with a top-of-mind position for certain products and brands – routing purchases were almost subconscious. Various – personal – reasons led to the initial product purchase, and this later became routine.

With recognizability, a more or less conscious choice is made, on the basis of price, recognizability or a top-of-mind position. It is, in fact, advertisements that have led to this position, but advertising and commercials also benefited from unambiguous recognizability (for instance, by means of the packaging) and repetition. Brands offered an excellent opportunity for this; after all, with a brand name you could unequivocally communicate via mass media to a mass audience that could buy the item in many places.

Additionally, on the basis of the product, a brand could also communicate such values as reliable, cosy or sexy. Brands have played an important role in advertising; the considerable growth seen in the advertising field can, to a large extent, be ascribed to the growth of branded items and the advertising budgets that were involved, but also to the product range policy of shops. Certain brands had to be included in the assortment in order to serve the customer, but also to create a positive atmosphere in the shop. Advertising outside shops selling branded goods is an example of this: if they sold that particular brand, then it had to be a good shop.

Brands were initially aimed at a mass supply for a large customer base; the grocery sector with all its variety was the right channel for this. Through the brand, manufacturers had a way of communicating with their customers directly, via mass media, and the reaction to a brand could be measured by means of market research and turnover. This development meant the advertising field became ever more important and increasingly more creative. Conveying values is a psychological process of creating atmosphere and invoking a memory at the moment of purchase. Associative values have to be in line with the product, the shop and the wishes of the customer. There are naturally plenty of examples: cigarettes that were portrayed as tough and adventurous, coffee that conveyed a convivial and homely atmosphere, and cars that emphasized the sexy image of the driver. Customers expressed a clear preference for brands.

> *CHICAGO (AdAge.com) – Facebook is preparing to launch location-based status updates for its users. But the social network is also planning to offer it to marketers, including McDonald's.*
>
> *As early as this month, the social-networking site will give users the ability to post their location within a status update. McDonald's, through digital agency Tribal DDB, Chicago, is building an app with Facebook which would allow users to check in at one of its restaurants*

and have a featured product appear in the post, such as an Angus Quarter Pounder, say executives close to the deal.

Facebook is not directly charging McDonald's to build the app; Facebook generally does not charge developers to build on its platform. But executives with knowledge say it was negotiated as part of a bigger media buy on Facebook, and McDonald's will be the first marketer to take advantage of the service.

The fast feeder won't be alone for long. While McDonald's is expected to be involved in the rollout in the next few weeks, execs at other digital shops have begun to spec out location-based campaigns in anticipation of Facebook's impending functionality, which will allow users to include their location in a status update.

San Francisco-based digital marketing firm Context Optional is working on Facebook location features for its retail clients. 'It's supposed to come out this month,' Context Optional CEO Kevin Barenblat said. 'So we're getting ready to incorporate it. We just don't know exactly when it's going to be available.'

Source: www.adage.co, 6 May 2010.

Alongside the brands in the grocery sector, more and more brands appeared in the non-food sector and the exclusive segment. Here again it was important to communicate unequivocally, but it was even more important to increase the product value, well above the intrinsic value of the products. Or, in other words, a customer was prepared to pay more for a branded item than for a non-brand item of identical value. This added value arose through the associative values that a customer assigned to the brand through advertising campaigns, but also through a stringent (advertising) policy: price, service, sales points and packaging, for example. Clothing brands, car makes and watch brands are good examples of this.

Manufacturers should build a personal relationship with their customers on the basis of the product, while the retailer can expand the relationship on the basis of personal contact, location or product range. In this context we then speak of building customer value. This customer value is defined as a multidimensional trade-off between what the customer gets (quality, benefits, image, security) and what he has to give to get this (such as the price). This perceived customer value is important in the purchasing process because the customer makes decisions based on this; is this product worth the money? In the first instance, customer value was sought in a product, which explains the rise of brands with a clearly perceived advantage. Later, the physical shop also acquired an important role in the generation of customer values. Nowadays the role played by the shop in respect of these customer values is such that stores (like Tesco and Sainsbury) are daring to compete against branded products. There is a large difference in this between the online shops and the existing physical shops: the difference between perception and physical experience.

The product itself makes little difference, customer appreciation is often tied to product characteristics and the perceived brand value.

In the 1970s and 1980s particularly, building product-linked brands was an important focal point and the advertising world was in its heyday. The change came in the 1990s. Consumers became worldlier due to greater mobility (holidays, business trips, car travel). Chain stores began to open in other countries and new markets and as a result their content became more mundane. A globalization of the business and identical patterns of consumption and products, as a result of people copying each other's behaviour, applied not only to retail chains, but increasingly to brands and products. Some people even talk of the Americanization of consumption and perhaps even more strikingly of McDonaldization.

As a result of this development, along with a strong drive for profit through new business models and other financing mechanisms (venture capital, private equity), the product ranges changed (there was an increasing focus on profitable products) as did the relationships with customers. Share of wallet, or rather trying to get the customer to spend as much as possible on your product or in your shop, became popular. The retailer also wanted to have an ever-larger share of the relevant budget, especially in combination with the increasing bond that was created with a shop or chain stores (even more than with a product). This is thus a battle between product loyalty (manufacturer) and shop loyalty. This battle has become increasingly intense, especially in recent years. Shops became stronger through the concentration of ownership, their expansion and the greater purchasing power as a result of this. The small shops were no longer able to buy in as cheaply as the large chains and thus experienced greater difficulties.

Loyalty

Customers are, in principle, loyal to a certain shop or product. Habit and trust are important reasons for this. However, the choice is also influenced by multidimensional values, in which image plays a role, as well as price and relationship with the product or shop. Naturally everybody likes the small shopkeeper, but at what price? The trade-off between rational factors like price and proximity and irrational factors such as image, appeal and trust is made very consciously by customers.

The combination of the power of the chain stores, the large range of items on offer and the intensive advertising linked to a low price means the small shopkeeper has in fact already lost the battle. However, a strong bond to the physical shop formula means consumers are loyal to the smaller stores. This bond and, in part, good legislation and strong consumer organizations, leads to an increased confidence in products. 'There aren't any bad products on sale anymore anyway' is the general feeling and the 'money back guarantee' provides extra confidence. This has resulted in the product brand becoming a commodity.

Thus dualism arises in customer value and customer relations: a relationship with shop formulas and a relationship with products. This dualism only really becomes a problem if shops with strong formulas no longer sell certain premium brands and will only promote their own-label items. This means customers have to choose and are left feeling that the shops are trampling over them in their battle. Customers are not happy with this, because having to make the choice between two of their preferences, branded goods and their favourite shop, will always lead to uncertainty.

Alongside the battle between products and shop formulas, there is also a fight going on between shop formulas and customer loyalty. In this, in addition to rational elements such as price, assortment and accessibility, experiential elements also play a strong role. Customers want to feel 'at home', feel they are being appealed to or made to feel special in order to buy in a shop. This battle is still going on and it is the customers who will determine the winner, which chain stores they choose, which channel they choose and which product. This applies equally to both food and non-food sectors.

The Advertising Industry Comes Under Pressure

The advertising field has also found things getting increasingly difficult. So many advertising mediums (newspapers, door-to-door advertising television, and so on) mean over-saturation has led to reduced attention and apathy to advertising. A large range of advertising media, advertising resources and advertising impulses led to customers being ever more difficult to reach; they were literally numbed by all the impulses. Customers also became more individualistic, markets fragmented, and target groups with identical customer groups grew ever smaller. It became more difficult to communicate advertising messages. Alongside these developments amongst customers and in the media, technology also became a significant factor for the advertising industry. Initially these were technological changes to direct communications such as folders and letters. Advertising customers, like manufacturers and chain stores, increasingly wanted to contact their customers directly; direct marketing became an integral component of advertising.

Direct marketing has the advantage that the effects can be measured by generating and measuring response. Through this the advertising agency can immediately see whether the advertising activity was successful. This became ever more important as a result of the greater focus on advertising and marketing costs and the uncertainty of the effect of advertising campaigns. Through direct marketing there was also a need to keep records of the names and addresses of customers, after all a follow-up letter might need to be sent or a brochure delivered. The introduction of the laser printer in 1981 made it possible to send personal letters to customers or potential customers. This at least gave a perception of personal contact.

The introduction of call centres and telemarketing at the beginning of the 1990s meant that advertisements were expanded from above the line, via mass media, to below the line through direct marketing and sales promotion. The advertising palette expanded even further and an area of tension arose between emotion and image, and ratio and response. This tension was perceptible in the advertising world but also led to confusion among manufacturers; the battle for the budget was more and more often a matter of an internal battle within the advertising agency driven by budgets and targets. Customers had no role in this; in fact, at the same time it was a battle for the customer. Advertisements were mostly product oriented, in which product values (or brand values) were communicated, but through direct marketing the ads were increasingly targeted at the individual needs of customers. Communication became direct, targeted, personal and based on a relationship.

This area of tension became even stronger in the 1990s through the outlined developments in the advertising world and through the individualization of demand. Customers were more mobile and more articulate, added to that were the technological possibilities, in advertising, in communications and naturally in terms of the phone and the Internet. The database with customers' names and addresses continued to grow in significance for direct communications at the end of the 1980s, but was also used at the beginning of the 1990s for direct telephone contacts, direct sales and customer services. When, in the middle of the 1990s, the first Internet applications appeared, the pressure on the advertising industry was so great that changes could no longer be held back. The era of unequivocal communication, based on products (brands) and mass communication had come to an end.

The Demand-driven Era

Direct marketing also marked the start of the demand-driven era. Individual demand, often in aggregated form, took centre stage. Everyone wants something different and after aggregation it appears that the target group (customers/buyers) is very diverse. Homogenous target groups in the classical sense (on the basis of objective characteristics) have disappeared, to be replaced by a group of individuals with a demand that can always change and which is sometimes defined by the moment. Entrepreneurs and advertising teams find it hard to reach this sort of customer. Individual wishes can be capitalized upon through interaction and by asking questions. This can be done on the Internet by analyzing the click-and-return behaviour. The behaviour of visitors to a site is automatically registered and can be analyzed. For the retailer with a traditional shop this is considerably more difficult. Discipline needs to be applied to ensure the purchasing details and name and address information of buyers are recorded and to ensure communication on this basis. In addition, a targeted interaction should arise at the moment of contact, where the retailer or their staff ask focused questions, so that good advice can be given about the purchase (transaction focus) and more knowledge about the customer is acquired.

This knowledge has to be recorded and the aim is focused communications. This method is new to the physical retail trade, as the moment of buying intention and completion of the transaction are important. The Internet provides another way of building a relationship that does not fit into the classic business model. The physical retailers still have a strong supply paradigm consisting of location, product range and personal relationship (the moment of contact). The advertising industry has always capitalized well on this by building brands, creating a top-of-mind position and approaching a large group of potential customers via mass media (see Figure 1.3, the supply-driven paradigm). The demand paradigm, in which individual demand is central, is new and calls for a different approach.

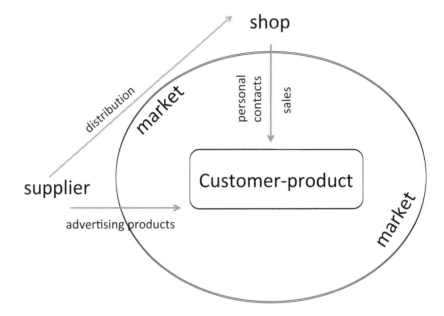

Figure 1.3   The supply-driven paradigm

Suppliers promote their products, they advertise to a mass market and sell through retailers. The personal contact is a relationship between customer and a shop(keeper). A customer has a relationship with the shop but also with the (branded) goods.

Product Brands Fight for a Future

Branded items also changed in the eyes of customers. Shops became brands, with extra brand values, especially in the grocery sector. Customers were more loyal to the shop and increasingly trusted the goods on offer. This offered shops the opportunity of offering private-label brands, the so-called own brands. The power of the private label is important in this respect.

PRIVATE LABELS AS GOOD ALTERNATIVES FOR A-BRANDS

Two-thirds of consumers world-wide consider own brands a good alternative to A-brands. For developed markets in Europe, the Pacific and North America this is the view of 80 per cent of consumers, as the latest Global Private Label Consumer survey by ACNielsen revealed.

In the survey, which is conducted online twice a year, ACNielsen asks consumers whether own brands in the supermarket are regarded as an alternative to other brands in terms of quality, value, packaging and positioning. The survey is conducted among 21,100 respondents in 38 countries in Europe, Asia Pacific, North America, Latin America and South Africa.

Source: Marketingonline, 15 August 2005.

If the shop is regarded as a strong brand, then its own brand will also be seen as strong and probably have the same values as a brand item. The association that the shop evokes will also be identical to the association of the own brand. Thus a chain of shops that is perceived to be 'cheap' will also have an own brand that customers regard as cheap. This shift from brand items to own brands is not only inspired by the price (cheaper) or a higher margin for the supplier, it is also a sign of the manufacturer adopting a different role in the relationship with the retailer. With the brand item, this was a collaborative role in which the retailer offered the items and often gave them a good position on the shelf, while the manufacturer took care of the advertising; a mutually beneficial agreement that offered added value to both parties and which was clear for the consumer.

Nowadays, shops have a strong bond with customers who see own labels as an integral component of the range on offer, and there is an imbalance in the relationship between the manufacturer and the shop. The first signs of this were perceptible in the 1990s, when the retailer started negotiating harder with manufacturers; the collaboration became more of a purchasing–supplier relationship. In particular, the market leaders (large chain stores) set tougher conditions in their buying policy; after all, wasn't it in the interests of the manufacturer that these items were sold by the shop? A fierce battle for the customer commenced: who has the bond with the customer? The shop or the branded item? In some cases the battle was perceptible, because retailers refused to sell certain products any longer. This initially related to specific products or products from a particular manufacturer, but some shops later decided to get rid of the entire product range. Under the pretext of having too many items or too little shelf space, a limited number of similar products were offered, with the own brand to the fore.

The lack of shelf space that subsequently became evident led to manufacturers being squeezed even more. Branded items had to be very strong if they were to survive this interplay of forces between manufacturers and retailers. In the end, it was the customer who determined who would win that much was true, but it wasn't very convincing. The shops would only come around and put more brand items on the shelves when there was a considerable drop in turnover.

It has become clear that manufacturers also face difficult choices. To keep the branded item, which could create a preferential choice for customers and enable a healthy margin, means advertising costs will rise due to the wealth of possibilities and the dilution of the impact. In addition, account must be taken of great pressure on the margin due to the strong negotiating position of the retailers. Another option is to use the production capacity to manufacture non-brand items and own brands. This could again lead to collaboration with the chain stores, but now in the role of manufacturer and customer. This could also have consequences for the margin, because the chain stores would have even more negotiating power; a fiendish dilemma.

Manufacturers Want Brands

One alternative for the manufacturer is direct sales. The items are then offered in their own shops or on the Internet. Nespresso and Apple, for example, have already opened shops; another well-known example are the pubs where beer brands have their own sales points and lease bars with contracts for the delivery of beer. It is also possible to order branded items directly on the Internet. This can be done via web-shops, where the owner of the online shop is not obvious, or directly from the manufacturer (Figure 1.4). Manufacturers are looking for new ways of making and maintaining contact with customers themselves and are prepared to develop new concepts and to try new sales channels. The retailer has the advantage of power, but it's not clear whether this advantage will also endure in the face of the current turbulence in markets and with the different buying behaviour of customers.

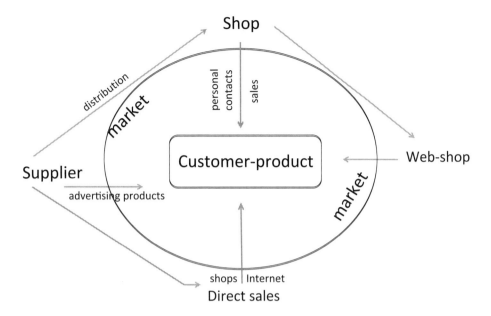

Figure 1.4   **Suppliers sell direct to customers by using their own shops or the Internet**

Non-food Brands

The development of brands outlined above is typical for the grocery sector. The brands are highly product-bound and are not directly linked to the manufacturer. A manufacturer can carry many brands and manufacture own labels as well. Large manufacturers like Unilever have hundreds of brands, each with its own appeal and target group. The real question is: to what extent are the physical products actually different? Blind tests by consumers often lead to indistinct preferences. It is precisely the perception of a brand that is important. Values are assigned to a product and product preference is defined on the basis of this perception.

In the non-food sector the appraisal is different. In this sector, large purchase sums are often involved and the brand is more strongly associated with experience and perception. A car make may technically be the same as a cheaper model, but thanks to design, accessories and brand emblem, still be perceived as radically different in the eyes of the customer. Of course, there may also be technical differences, but through the transparency of the market and the integral application of technology these differences are getting smaller and smaller, although they do still exist.

Watches, clothing and mobile phones have the same recognizability and customers also have a clear preference. Own labels do not really exist in the luxury sector. It's precisely that element of luxury, spoiling oneself, allowing yourself to have it, that is more important than the rational side. Chanel No. 5 is not the same as some unknown perfume, a Jaeger Le Coultre watch is not the same as an unknown brand. Some people like to associate themselves with the prestigious brands and would rather buy a fake version of it rather than an unbranded product.

Brand manufacturers are also noticing the change in purchasing behaviour as consumers have more money to spend and want to distinguish themselves from the rest. Although the move to individualization is an important development, a feeling of belonging can not be wiped out among certain groups of consumers. Motorbike riders greet each other, drivers of the same make of car feel a bond, and the wearers of a luxury watch brand feel they have a common affinity. A brand item indicates that you belong, or wish to belong to a certain group; it makes you different. These sorts of brands profit from current developments in the market. It is only in the case of a continuing recession that customers might purchase a cheaper alternative or postpone their purchase. On the other hand, if you see people parading around in poor countries with Nike shoes and shirt, it's clear that brands can also be used there to make a statement!

> **THE CRISIS HAS NOT CHANGED THE PREFERENCE FOR BRANDS**
>
> *The economic recession has hardly had any effect on the confidence the people have in well-known brands. Just like last year 62% of people prefer to use a Nokia mobile phone, 39% have a preference for petrol from Shell and the favourite telecom company of 53% of the population is the former state owned telco-operator, (like BT) as the European Trusted Brands survey conducted by Reader's Digest revealed. Nokia phones have been the favourites for nine years. Just like last year, Kellogg's and Shell are also among the top five most trusted brands.*

Source: Nu.nl, 6 May 2009.

The Retail Challenge is Called 'the Internet'

The retail trade is traditionally dependent on consumers. Shops were opened near to their target market group and the range of goods on offer was adapted to the expected demand. Every morning the shop door was opened and the shopkeeper waited for customers, who did in fact come. Location and product range were the traditional entrepreneur/shopkeeper's weapons of competition, and this is still true for physical shops; very strongly supply oriented and waiting for passers-by and customers. This is an extremely passive approach to retail trading. However, customer buying behaviour has changed substantially in recent years without the retail trade having effectively capitalized on this.

> Year on year, the volume of retail sales in March was 2.2 per cent higher than in March 2009. Predominantly food stores decreased by 0.8 per cent while predominantly non-food stores increased by 6.7 per cent. Within predominantly non-food stores there were rises for all sectors, the largest being non-specialised stores at 8.7 per cent. Non-store retailing increased by 13.9 per cent.

Source: UK National Statistics.

The non-store sales were mainly in the non-food segment, the very retailer who is now at risk of going under. This turnover, on top of all the changes already mentioned, has a direct effect on the turnover of the regular shops.

The Internet has a strong influence on consumer buying behaviour; all of a sudden there is an opportunity to buy from the comfort of your own home. At present, 80 per cent of the population of west-European countries have direct access to a (fast) Internet connection. Of these, 70 per cent indicate that they have, at one time or another, bought something on the Internet and have had a good experience doing so. With new methods of payment, such as Paypal, and more security from the consumer watch authorities, the Internet has become a good alternative to the time-honoured physical act of shopping (Table 1.3).

Table 1.3   Growth in online sales in Europe

2006	+6.4%
2007	+8.6%
2008	+10.2%
2009	+11.6%

Source: GFK Retail and Technology, April 2010.

Retailers often complain that the Internet leads to unfair competition because of the low prices and low costs. However, that would mean that consumers always make a buying decision based on price and that is certainly not the case. The reasons for consumers (also) buying on the Internet are also often very personal.

- You can shop whenever you want. Online shopping is mainly done on rainy days and Sundays. Those are the days that people can find shopping in regular stores a problem. Current national shop trading house are very restrictive for the shops; whilst consumers want to be able to shop on Sundays, or maybe in the evening after work, the shops are not allowed to open. Sometimes bad weather is blamed for a reduction in sales figures, but the same has actually led to an increase in Internet sales. Web shopping is obviously complementary to physical shopping and has therefore become a fully-fledged alternative.

- The ease and the service. Customers can easily exchange items that have been bought on the Internet. Thus items are ordered, calmly approved and/or tried on and, if necessary, sent back without any worries and without any pressures from sales staff. It's precisely this ease that is a stimulus to buying more. In a shop the sales staff are sometimes found to be annoying and incompetent. On the Internet it's possible to calmly buy without feeling pressured, and all the necessary information can be found on the retailer's website or by Googling. The retail trade consequently loses the role of expert. An added value (higher price) for the advice is then illogical, after all customers often know more about the products or the use thereof than the sales staff in the shop. With the current pressure on margins, economies are also being made when it comes to staffing; there are fewer staff and they are less competent. This in turn means that customers will go to physical shops even less often and do their own research on the Internet. The trust in the knowledge of the shop personnel is gone. The reason for still going to the shop at all is the fact that the items are there (for a physical check) and can be taken away immediately.

- The knowledge and service. Customers have acquired knowledge of the product via weblogs or by Googling. They also know what prices are being asked by looking on the web and often also at foreign web-shops. If the price online is different to the prices asked by the regular retail trade the customer will not accept that. Some 10 per cent of customers now consider it acceptable to negotiate the price of more expensive items. Through the Internet, customers know what an item should cost and they don't want to pay any more than necessary. The retail trade is generally inclined to concede to this negotiation, because they are unable to indicate why a customer in the shop should pay more for items than on the Internet. Guarantees are also given by web-shops, the item can be returned, there is a home shopping warranty and the items are delivered to the customer's home.

- The communications. Retailers don't know their customers, and know little about their customers and their needs. Any customer entering the shop is regarded as a buy signal. No questions are asked about backgrounds or needs and the customer's name is rarely known. Communication takes place via advertisements in the local press or via a conversation in the shop. This is not really personal. Web-shops should know the customer, even if it's only to be able to dispatch the goods and arrange the payment. This makes it possible to communicate directly (via e-mail) and to respond to visits and buying behaviour; there is a perceived personal relationship. This is evident with Amazon.com which makes suggestions for items on the basis of historic purchasing and search behaviour. Companies like landsend.com, sport sites and many other retail outlets have copied this. Although the customer knows that it's an automatically generated e-mail message, he responds positively to it. The physical retail trade rarely makes use of e-mail, the Internet or customer data. They consequently remain dependent on the moment that the customer walks into the shop.

There will also be a struggle for life on the Internet, and only those web shops that capitalize on the opportunities and possibilities offered by the Internet and respond to customer requirements will survive. I realized this when I booked a trip to Africa with my travel agent. Even though it was late evening, I received answers to my questions by e-mail within ten minutes. I was kept constantly informed about what they were checking out for me and they gave me feedback by e-mail. The comfortable feeling that I was being kept up to date with the process, that I could contact them whenever it suited me and that

my trip really was being tailored to my wishes, made me realize that
this is the future for Internet shopping. Especially now web shops
should capitalize on meeting the wishes of individual customers
and communicate at times that suit the customer. The perception of
customised work is the next step in the evolution of shopping.

Source: Twinkle, January 2009.

There is a countermovement however; customers don't always want to shop at home, rationally and functionally. Having a day out is also good for people. In particular, mobility enables people to experience new things, to be amused. However, there has to be a reason, a shop opening, an attractive shopping street, a fair or a sale. Shopping has (due in part to the Internet) joined the list of leisure activities for the people strolling round the shops on a Saturday and ending up with a relaxing drink at a pavement café or a Starbucks. However, this doesn't always work to the advantage of the retailer. Parking problems and costs, and local council policy are seldom beneficial to the retail trade.

Starbucks adds to the fun of shopping. In London alone they have opened 260 coffee shops in recent years. But coffee shops, and other leisure places, are a normal part of the high street nowadays.

Starbucks' UK and Ireland chief executive Darcy Willson-Rymer said
the failure of high street retailers had opened up new opportunities for
the chain to open branches where it does not yet have a presence.

Mr Willson-Rymer said the company could pick up key retail sites at
bargain prices because the recession has caused the first drop in retail
rents since the since the early nineties.

Mr Schultz said: 'We're not only here to stay but our best days are
ahead of us especially in the UK, where it's still early for us. We've
great confidence in our business here and we're going to continue to
grow the market.'

There are already 260 Starbucks branches in Greater London.

Source: *Daily Telegraph*, 27 March 2009.

Customers then look for ways of shopping recreationally in places and at locations where shopping is still fun and parking is easy. IKEA is a good example of this: long opening hours, good parking facilities, something for the inner man (and woman), and attractions for the kids, with no limits on walking around, looking and trying. A day out to IKEA is a day out for the whole family. Traffic jams on the motorway are simply regarded as an unavoidable inconvenience. In marketing we call this experience marketing. We see the same with Mediamarkt, an 'Alice in Wonderland' for men. Everything is out on display for potential buyers to try; nothing is behind glass or in cases. Here too we see long opening hours and no parking problems. These large retail chains demonstrate a development in retail trade in which an appealing formula will push small retailers out of business, as has happened in the USA with Wal-Mart. Until now Wal-Mart has not been successful in transferring their concept to Europe, but should this happen one day, the misery for the current retail trade would simply be immense! The answer lies in the customers who see shopping as recreation. Internet shopping remains very functional and boring. Offer an advantage that is not boring, predictable and rational and the customers will keep coming!

Shopping has to be fun and carefree and also surprising, just try that in most shops. If shopping can no longer be fun – emotional – it becomes rational. And rational shopping can be done many times better on the Internet (Table 1.4).

Table 1.4   Most popular websites in the UK in 2009

Social network	Web-shops	Software	Small ads
Myspace.com	Amazon.co.uk	Microsoft.com	Loot.com
Facebook.com	Play.com	Adobe.com	Gumtree.com
Bebo.com		Apple.com	
Flickr.com		Wordpress.com	

Source: Flamenewmedia.com.

In addition, personal motives also play a role with consumers: the pressures of family life felt by double-income couples (between 30 and 50), the pressure on quality time and the need to spend a lot of time and energy with the children. There is barely any time for shopping, and shopping with children is far from fun. All things considered, there is a lot of pressure on the retail trade, but they also have to search their own consciences. As Darwin concluded back in 1856, after his visit to the Galapagos Islands, it is not the biggest or the strongest that will survive, but those who are most able to adapt to the circumstances.

Is the Internet a Threat to the Shop?

The first reaction of the retail trade to the Internet was an extremely defensive one. Suppliers were supposed to apply a different price for sales via the Internet to sales via their own shops. Retailers had the costs of a building, inventory and stocks and were thus placed in a negative competitive position compared to Internet companies. The extra costs of a web-shop were not appreciated. Running a web-shop is not cheap, as we will see later, its just that the costs are not so obvious.

Suppliers consequently used a so-called dual pricing strategy, whereby regular retailers were charged a lower purchase price than web retailers. The suppliers were afraid of the consequences from the distribution channel and thus artificially kept the retail trade alive, although in fact it was fast asleep. Now that sales volumes via the Internet are rising sharply (expected to be 33 per cent of non-food retail sales within five years) the balance of power is changing. Additionally, web-shops are also finding other purchasing channels via parallel imports and other suppliers, but foreign web-shops also are happy to deliver to anywhere in the world. Purchasing goods from America is now just as easy as buying from France, Holland or England. This protection of the existing retail trade is only a temporary measure and certainly doesn't solve the problem.

> More and more Europeans have access to the Internet. Some 56 per cent of the inhabitants of the 27 European member states are online.
>
> This emerged from a survey conducted by the European Commission. In comparison to 2004 the number of people using the Internet has increased by a third. Half of all European households and 80 per cent of all businesses have a broadband connection. Most Internet users are under 24 years of age. In this age category 66 per cent are online every day. Of the remaining Internet users in the EU, 43 per cent are online every day and the survey also revealed that young people do not want to pay for services online. Three quarters of the young people between 16 and 24 admit that they have at some time downloaded illegally. In addition 33 per cent of young people do not want to pay for online information. Both percentages are twice as high for young people as for the rest of the European Internet users.

Source: ANP, 5 August 2009.

Selling Through the Internet

Table 1.5   Household access to the Internet in 2008

All households	86%
Single person households	71%
Single parent families	87%
Families without children	91%
Families with children	98%

Source: CBS, the Netherlands; figures for 2008. Figures of Western European countries are comparable.

Retail traders can take measures themselves. They could start selling via the Internet, as smaller shops are already doing. There are examples in the sports world, where sports foods and clothing can also be bought online. In addition to the physical shop, a retailer can also run a very successful web-shop. The fact that there is also a physical shop gives even more confidence and trust to buyers. Even hairdressers have discovered a new target group on the Internet. On their websites they offer haircare products and advice on hair growth. Customers come from all over the country in some cases to speak to the hairdresser personally.

> *The BCSC indicate that whilst online retailing will exert pressure on retail rental growth over the next five to ten years, this will be felt most acutely in smaller centres. Larger shopping centres will remain desirable destinations in which to shop, and are deemed virtually immune to the impact of online shopping. Physical stores will remain the most popular point of sale for retailers and expansions are set to continue, although greater use of websites will be made as a means of distributing goods to customers.*

Source: www.Wigan.gov.uk.

It's also possible to make use of existing web-shops, through an affiliate programme. Popular shops with a lot of visitors can offer other companies a space to open a web-shop. This enables them to profit from the web traffic of the host web-shop and from the existing logistics process. This way, shopping malls are created on the Internet where it's possible to link up with sites that have a lot of traffic. eBay is developing a trading platform in which retail traders can offer items or can place links to their shop. As a result they come into contact with potential customers who are still in the orientation phase. This also means that the customer will involve this shop in his orientation and have a reason for going to the shop. The retailer is then no longer passively waiting for customers, but is actively guiding customers to his shop. The bookshop group Selexyz has introduced another successful change. By giving all books a radio-frequency identification (RFID) tag[1] they have been able to streamline and monitor the purchasing process, to do stocktaking more often and define which books are selling fast and which not so well. Direct customer support in the buying process is possible as a terminal in the shop can indicate whether a book is in stock and if so, where it can be found. It's also possible to make suggestions for other books, in the same way as can be done online at Amazon.co.uk.

The future impact of a rise in Internet shopping remains unclear, however it is evident that the growth in e-commerce will affect some sectors more than others (see Figure 1.5). For example, consumers are more likely to shop online for electrical items than clothing. However, the British Council of Shopping Centres (BCSC) note that e-tailing will never replace the shopping experience, and the impetus is for retailers to create a comfortable environment for shoppers to attract them.

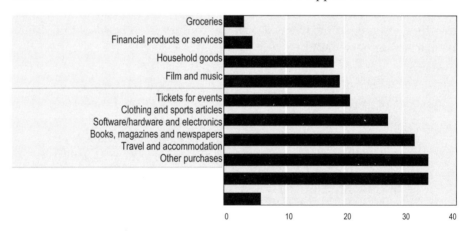

Figure 1.5   People who made electronic purchases in the last 12 months
Source: Extracted from CBS: the figures relate to the turnover in 2006. The graph is mainly intended to show the difference between the various branches in respect of competition from the Internet.

---

1   Radio-frequency identification (RFID) is the use of an object (typically referred to as an RFID tag) applied to or incorporated into a product, animal, or person for the purpose of identification and tracking using radio waves. Some tags can be read from several metres away and beyond the line of sight of the reader. Information can be stored on the RFID tag (chip), such as history, price, ingredients.

The retail trade is correctly sounding the alarm bell but it must look for the cause of the expected problems in the field itself. The change from a supply-driven approach to a demand-driven approach demands other skills and a different use of technology. Being more efficient is only a partial solution, as is retailing on the Internet. It calls for an approach that starts from the new consumer with a different buying behaviour and other preferences. New market circumstances must be exploited, in a way that suits the company, the goods on offer and the intended customers. Passively waiting for customers and competing with location and product range is totally inadequate for survival. Nowadays customers buy in a different way, they know more than they used to and make different demands of shops and of shopping. It is thus a case of adapting to survive. However, a reorganization of the retail outlet, because customers want to buy in a different way, is also part of a healthy economic process.

Buying Behaviour

Before the purchase, information is sought at product level about the product, the price, experiences of other users and availability. Videos are viewed and weblogs consulted. In chat rooms other people can be consulted. The intensity of this phase is highly dependent on the product, the level of experience with the Internet, and often the age of the person. Most Internet users search via Google for the product and information about it. Users and shops in the local vicinity are sought via small ads sites and eBay. Weblogs are not often used anymore because they are seen as being too subjective. It is therefore important for product suppliers to appear in Google and Yahoo with the right entry and in the right place. Physical retailers must have an entry on information sites and trading sites like eBay, and they also have to be easy to find. Potential buyers search for the product but they also want to be able to buy it somewhere. All that takes on the Internet is a single click, for physical shops it's a bit trickier. Customers have to come to you in the shop. As we've seen, this happens in specific cases in order to reduce uncertainty, or if you want to have the item quickly (buy and take it with you). At that point in time the competitive battle is actually fought most keenly; is the customer going to buy something right now from a web-shop or will the purchase be delayed until it can be bought in a shop (see Table 1.6)?

Table 1.6   The difference between physical buying and buying on the
               Internet

BUYING BEHAVIOUR PRODUCT	PHYSICAL	VIRTUAL
Ratio	Advantage of ease and low price perception	With a larger choice on the Internet there is an advantage of ease and price
Emotion	Especially physical, through buying experience and environment, shop furnishing and atmosphere	Emotion is difficult to evoke, only for virtual products like games, dating and music
Shopping goods	Seeing, feeling, smelling, trying products Depending on shop and personnel a purchase is made	Searching for information on the Internet is easier but physical control is desired With experience, less and less physical control will be required
Convenience goods	You bump into it, it mustn't take much effort	You are confronted with it and buy directly from a known retailer. If no risk is perceived a purchase is made

Briefing

Customers are buying differently nowadays. Physical shopping takes place for clear reasons such as the social contact, being able to take products home straight away and being able to feel, smell and try on the products.

Customers are buying more and more on the Internet and also use the Internet to find information. Before a customer enters a shop he is already fully aware of the possibilities and the prices. Often the customer will already have chosen a particular product but still wants to see it. Sales staff must have specialized knowledge and social and communicative skills. A visitor to the shop has buying intentions, but if he walks away then the salesman has not interpreted them well. The price is only one part of the buying motives; trust, good contact and service are just as important (see Table 1.7).

In the future customers will buy at a time that suits them. More than ever before, retailers need to motivate customers to buy from them. Customers want to feel special. Retailers should get to know the customer well and build a relationship using all the means that the customer prefers.

Table 1.7   **Advantages and disadvantages of physical shopping versus web shopping**

	Web-shop	Physical shop
Advantages	Interactive customer contact, customer details immediately known, lots of knowledge about interaction and visitors, immediate payment, trust through the home shopping warranty. Intention to buy and buying coincide.	Items in the shop, can be taken away immediately, personal contact, locally in stock, ambience, feeling and emotion in the shop. Emotional loyalty possible.
Disadvantages	Items have to be supplied, uncertainty through unfamiliarity, often payment in advance, uncertainty about products (sometimes) and about the shop. Technical barrier, problems finding one's way around the site. How do you find the shop the first time or on subsequent occasions if you haven't saved it as a bookmark?	Physical limitations such as parking or personnel who you don't like, item not in stock, personnel who don't know you, impersonal, delivery to home often takes a long time, taking purchases with you can be difficult, still not much service. Time delay between buying intention and actual purchase.

UK Top Comparison Sites

1. Kelkoo.co.uk – features a large number of categories including books, CDs, travel, computing and electronics categories. (Kelkoo also run Shopgenie).

2. Pricerunner UK – covers many categories from books, through electrical appliances to travel insurance.

3. Shopping.com UK – offers a large number of categories, from appliances, through music to jewellery. Shopping.com also runs the sites Dealtime and DoorOne.

4. Ciao.co.uk – comparisons and reviews across a wide range of categories.

5. Google's Product Search service – with ordering by price (unfortunately no postage info is included) and breakdown by category.

6. Amazon.co.uk – not often thought of as a comparison site, but features prices from other retailers alongside its own prices.

7. BuyCentral.co.uk – offers a categorized and searchable database of products, that can be ordered and filtered by price.

8. Pricegrabber UK – limited to PC goods and consumer electrical equipment.

9. Nextag UK – offers a wide variety of categories.

10. Shopping.zdnet.co.uk – PC goods, digital cameras and camcorders.

11. Shopzilla.co.uk – covers a wide range of categories, from clothing to video games and cosmetics.

Not a Lot Has Changed in 45 years; the Basic Principles Still Apply!

WHY DO PEOPLE BUY?

If we are able to answer this question, we can gauge a customer's attitude and use this knowledge to make the sale transaction easier for the retailer and more satisfying for the shopper. There are several fundamental motives which explain why people buy:

1. The satisfaction of physical needs. *Food, drinks and clothing are necessities of life and are universally in demand, but much more is demanded of merchandise than the mere fulfilling of man's basic need for survival. Hence, consumers require, in addition, that food and drink shall be attractive in appearance and taste, also convenient to prepare and cook; similarly, clothing must be smart and durable, as well as warm.*

2. Recreation and comfort. *The greater purchasing power of a large proportion of the population and the shorter working weeks have made the sale of merchandise which will satisfy this need much more important in recent years. Examples*

include sports equipment, toys and games, as well as labour-saving equipment and luxuries for domestic or personal use.

3.   Imitation. *People in general wish to imitate those whom they admire, or whose tastes are considered superior. Vast sales of cosmetics, toilet preparations for men and women and clothing are made because of this desire.*

4.   Exclusiveness. *In contrast to those who wish to imitate, many people wish to be distinctive, to be different, or to be the leaders in fashion. They will be willing to pay high prices for model garments and hand-made furniture, for example, so that they can maintain their prestige in the eyes of those around them.*

Family affection. The need and pleasure of children attract a large amount of spending by parents but in addition to this, the pleasure derived from gift giving in general is a powerful motive which can be used to great advantage by the retailer. Other motives which induce people to buy include: Health, Habit, Curiosity, Novelty, Possession and Pride.

Source: Thomas, P.G. *Modern Retailing Techniques*, Macdonald and Evans Ltd, London 1963, p. 116.

2

A New Way of Shopping: The Role of Customer Experience and Entertainment

Buying is not just a rational process, it also often involves emotions, personal preferences or environmental influences (a seductive store layout, music and so on). Buying nowadays is more a combination of ratio with experience, and perhaps even a bit of entertainment. This also applies to the day-to-day purchases made in the supermarket. Product demonstrations, a coffee shop, a reading corner or a magazines section, it's all part of the game these days – grocery shopping should be fun too.

From a supply perspective (sales are transactions) shops aim at rational buying motives: price, range on offer, personal contact and, perhaps, parking facilities. The supply perspective is based on a retailer who thinks from within their business model: more transactions, a good margin and acceptable profits. The focus on transactions is extremely dominant in this approach. The moment of buying, picking up on buying signals and motivating people to buy are important components of the sale and entrepreneurs often have a good feeling about it. If all customers were the same and had the same buying motives then this approach would be favourable. Once a customer enters the shop they have to be paid attention to, assisted and motivated to make a purchase. In the past, customers have had a limited choice of shops and products. Their action radius was confined and they never knew what was on sale where and at what price. The customer entering the shop was the 'moment suprême' for the retailer. Selling was 'effecting a transaction'.

This traditional, transaction-oriented approach has come under pressure through external changes (exogenous factors) such as the use of the Internet and, partly as a consequence of that, changes in customer buying behaviour: a different leisure experience, pressure on how double-income families spend their spare time, mobility and social commitments. In the previous chapter we looked at these changes from an external perspective, in this chapter we focus on the behaviour of customers and potential customers. Customers are individualistic, self-willed and have their own preferences and motives. It's difficult for the retailer to read into them. More than ever before, selling is about listening to and communicating with the customer. This means not performing a 'hard sell' and continually pushing the advantages of a product, but rather responding to buying motives and working on building a continuing relationship. If customers buy something this is not a process of successive transactions, but an intrinsic feeling of being given pleasure and feeling comfortable in the shop. For customers this is logical; retailers still have to get used to this, but it will determine their future.

Rational versus Emotional Purchases

Rational purchases are made on the basis of necessity. Many food purchases are rational; people look at the product on the shelf, the price and perhaps the ingredients. Customers often also prefer to make purchases in shops that are local to them, offer parking facilities or services that appeal (like home delivery or payment in instalments). However, in the food sector, habit and routine also play an important role; you know where to find everything and always buy the same product in the same packaging. Routine is an important buying motive for customers. When the packaging of a product is changed, or if the products are put in a different place in the shop, customers find it irritating. They will be inclined to give up because they've lost their routine, or get annoyed and go to a different shop. Rational-based loyalty means that any bond is based on rational elements only. As soon as a different supplier scores better on these elements the customer is gone. It is therefore difficult to build up an enduring relationship on rational grounds.

A low price is nice, but perhaps there are other suppliers who are able to offer an even lower price because they require a lower margin or simply have lower costs. This is a constant battle for the customers' favour, but loyalty is based on more than just rational thinking and customers will rarely buy simply on the basis of these motives. If it's a matter of necessity then it does happen, of course: if a customer urgently needs a packet of cigarettes or a carton of milk then they will do all they have to do to buy it, even if that means going to a different shop, or buying a different brand. Many household products also belong in this category; everyday articles and consumables. This can vary from a hairdryer to a purchase as large as a washing machine. Many people don't know the brand name of their washing machine and interest is only aroused if necessary. That's why there is more brand preference for umbrella brands, brands that many products belong to, than for brands with a single product. Philips and Sony are typical umbrella brands. The recognition and positive association with the brand is then greater. It's not until the product has to be repaired or replaced that people look at the brand again. With a positive experience there will again be a preference for the same brand, provided the price and performance (perception) are in proportion and provided the sales staff don't contradict this. The brand loyalty and emotion in respect of household appliances are limited, but in the eyes of the customer these are nevertheless necessary products. They mustn't cause any problems; they just need to work properly. As long as the product has always functioned properly, consumers will show a preference for the brand (women often have a preference for the same brand as their mother; experience with the product and faith in their mother is great).

Table 2.1   **Customer satisfaction scores for the top UK pure-play online retailers, December 2009**

Amazon UK	83
Play.com	79
QVC UK	78
Apple.com UK	76
M&M Direct	76
eBay UK	75
ASOS	74
Ebuyer	74
La Redoute	67
Dixons	66

Source: Foresee Results (Likemind Survey), December 2009.

Such findings confirm that the online shopping channel is firmly embedded in the public consciousness, and that e-tailers are doing things right and producing satisfied customers. Perhaps more important is the evidence that, even in difficult economic times, shoppers care about more than just price – two-thirds of respondents in the Likemind survey said they would be turned off of making a purchase by poor service – and are looking at the full picture of what retailers can provide (see Table 2.1).

'Online merchants need to look beyond price and convenience,' said eMarketer Senior Analyst Karin von Abrams. 'These have been key drivers of online shopping growth in the past, along with the rising number of consumers using the Internet and having positive experiences online.'

'But online stores will increasingly be defined and differentiated by their standards of service – especially when the overall rate of growth is slowing,' she said.

Improving customer service also gives e-tailers the opportunity to appeal to customer segments that may have been overlooked. Consumers who particularly value conscientious, reliable service typically include those with higher incomes and older people whose expectations of service were formed before the age of the Web.

Likemind said the respondents most likely to consider service better online were those ages 55 and older, many of whom have not yet adopted online shopping with the zeal of younger groups.

Keep your business ahead of the digital curve.

Source: www.emarketer.com.

Despite all the logical motives, people still base their purchases on a combination of ratio and emotion. Customers feel a bond with the shop or product. This bond can consist of placing the purchase order, or it may be a personal bond because the salesperson is pleasant and friendly or because you know the owner personally. Often this bond is not sufficiently recognized by the retailer, and only the (low) price is taken into account to indicate the bond with the customer. The Internet is therefore considered a threat, because the prices can be lower on account of the lower running costs. This will lead to a price-based clash which the physical retailer can never win. If customers start buying on price alone then their fate is decided. The current move on the part of retailers to join this price war is understandable, but incorrect; customers have many more motives for buying than the price alone!

TESCO, WAL-MART AND THE REST

The price weapon is often used in the groceries sector. A few years ago there was a direct price war between the various supermarket chains. Tesco is market leader and has more shops than other grocers, therefore they have more buying power with the supplier. It seems logical that because of the scale of operation they can be more competitive than other grocers. But there is more. Because grocery is a daily need, you can not live without your supermarket. This loyalty can be transferred to more products and more services. If you walk into a Tesco supermarket nowadays you realize that the days of a store just offering groceries are long past. Through their lower prices, Tesco and Wal-Mart suddenly became interesting to a larger consumer group. These stores offered not only low prices but also a one-stop shopping experience. The consumer could visit these stores not only for their groceries but many more of their daily needs such as toys, clothing and tools. Tesco won over the customers that had previously purchased these goods at Woolworths. The end result is clear.

Loyalty – Where Do We Buy?

Loyalty on emotional grounds is stronger than loyalty on financial grounds (price). Loyalty also demonstrates a preference for brands, products or shops that represent extra value for the customer. Customers buy on emotional as well as rational grounds. Customer relations consists of three components.

First there is the financial connection, usually based on price. Low prices create a bond, but as soon as consumers see a lower price elsewhere they will soon transfer this loyalty. Loyalty based on price is not a long-lasting loyalty. 'Low-price hunters' are always looking for discounts, both in the real world and on the Internet. A retailer will have great difficulty retaining these customers or making a good margin on them. They hop from shop to shop and from product to product. Fighting this is a waste of energy, clever customers will always find cheaper shops and cheaper products – even if the quality and the reliability is debatable – and off they go again.

Social loyalty involves more emotional aspects. Customers want to belong to a particular group, buy products to identify with that group and buy from shops that strengthen that group feeling. Car drivers feel this very strongly about their make of car. A Mercedes driver is not a Skoda driver and a Tesco customer is a different sort of person to someone who shops at Waitrose. A social bond can also arise because customers regard a retailer or a product as pleasant or agreeable, or because there are positive product associations based on, for example, environmental aspects, or because it's used by celebrities. If retailers are also congenial, or personally known to the customer (maybe through their football, bridge or rotary club), then the customer will not begrudge the retailer his turnover. It is therefore important for entrepreneurs to also take this into account when selecting their staff; they are the company's calling card so to speak, and can make or break the social bond. Customers have to feel comfortable and thus give the entrepreneur their custom, that is, the turnover.

Finally, there is also a structural bond that arises through routine and habit (as happens in the supermarket and also on the Internet). Customers get used to navigating around and to the look and feel of a particular website. It is daring to deviate from this, after all, once the routine is broken, a customer may look elsewhere and there is plenty of choice out there. Another form of structural loyalty is contractual: the contract with a mobile operator, an Internet service provider or in the form of all kinds of subscriptions. Leaving is not an option, a contract is a contract. Through the contract period there is also a period of (forced) commitment, and routine and habit occur as a matter of course. If the retailer doesn't go too far, customers will remain loyal for that very reason. Existing companies have an easier time than newcomers in that respect. 'Why leave BT, they've always been so good?' Stopping only causes a lot of bother and for what?

In the 1970s, the Bijenkorf department store in The Netherlands was having problems and was at risk of having to close its shops. Because the Dutch people considered this a big loss, people suddenly started buying en masse at the Bijenkorf and there were even protest campaigns held – the Bijenkorf has to stay! And the Bijenkorf stayed. This was in sharp contrast to the developments in the UK with Woolworths, where the loyalty shown by consumers was not enough to keep the company profitable.

The Downfall of Woolworths[1]

One of the UK's largest retailers, Woolworths, had been in business for 99 years and 6 months when it had to close its doors, just before Christmas 2008. The downfall of Woolworths actually occurred in stages: the takeover by equity

---

1   Source: *Daily Telegraph*, 2 February 2009.

funds that wanted an interest reimbursement on their investments and the disposal of the shop buildings in a 'sale and leaseback' construction, for which high rents had to be paid. Even during the good years, prior to the recession, the profit margin was only 1–2 per cent. When the turnover fell by several per cent, because of the recession and the stiffer competition, Woolworths soon found themselves in a loss situation. This resulted not only in a lack of financial resources, but also a lack of trust amongst their suppliers. The goods were not selling fast enough to be able to pay for new stocks. Because Woolworths no longer owned the building their stores were located in, and were being charged high rents, high interest rates meant the company's fate was soon decided. In the run up to Christmas 2008, stock was sold at huge discounts and the shops closed; a clear sign of change.

Investment in stock is necessary for the physical retail trade, after all customer want to see, feel, try, buy and take their purchases with them immediately. The Woolworths brand and the power of consumer confidence were not enough to beat the competition. In fact the rational buying motives were stronger than the emotional motives so that other shops (Tesco) and other channels (the Internet) were enough to make customers buy there instead. But the Woolworths brand is strong and many British people feel a bond with it. In February 2009, two entrepreneurs decided to buy the Woolworths brand and to use it to sell via the Internet. This meant they could capitalize on the brand value of Woolworths without immediately having to invest in buildings and stock. A revival of Woolworths, in a new environment, is underway.

WOOLWORTHS IS TO BE REBORN ONLINE

The Woolworths brand is to be re-launched as an online retailer after being bought by Daily Telegraph owners, Sir David and Sir Frederick Barclay. The much-loved High Street chain went into administration in November and its more than 800 stores closed a month ago after struggling with debts of £385m.

Shop Direct Group bought the Woolworths brand in February after the high street chain fell into administration last year. The company relaunched Woolworths as an online brand over the summer. As well as buying Woolworths, Shop Direct also owns the Ladybird brand, which was formerly owned by Woolworths Group.

Source: *Daily Telegraph*, 2 February 2009.

Functional and Hedonistic Shopping

The difference between rational and functional is small. Rational relates to the fact that rational choices are made, often choices based on logic. These considerations could include parking places at shopping centres, the possibility of visiting different shops, home delivery services and perhaps a one-stop shopping concept. Being functional is about efficient shopping; being able to find articles quickly and leave again quickly. Functional shopping takes place in stores where it's easy to get around the shop fast and with few hold-ups. This way of shopping isn't fun but it is effective. Either way, it's not so much the prices that are the deciding factor but other aspects; this is therefore in contrast to rational shopping. The Internet is also ideal for functional shopping provided the site has a logical layout and navigation structure. If you've been on the site before, you will know your way around and this makes it really efficient. Efficiency and routine influence each other. You can shop efficiently if, through your routine, you know exactly where you can find everything and what the best times are for shopping. Efficient shopping is especially important when it comes to groceries. For many people doing the grocery shopping is not exactly their highlight of the day. This should be taken into account when designing the layout of the shop (and the location). Although functional shopping is often associated with grocery shopping and with the Internet, there is no mutual stimulation. Online grocery shopping does happen but will always make up a limited percentage of the purchases (3 per cent at most). This has to do with the nature of the groceries, freshness of the products and nearby shops with the convenience of collecting them personally.

Home delivery (including the 'pick n pack' service) costs money and therefore either requires a minimum spend or delivery charges. Home delivery services are primarily popular in regions with families with double incomes and those with small children (especially for the purchase of heavy items). In these cases, the efficiency aspect is very personal. Small shopkeepers in villages will still deliver to elderly people and people with small children as part of the (local) service. This old service is now implemented in a modern way with shopping on the Internet. Efficiency is mostly associated with necessary groceries, sometimes it's also to do with an aversion to shopping per se. Men often have an aversion to shopping, they will therefore choose a shop where they know for certain that they will find something they like so that they don't have to look anywhere else. Clothing shops know this and capitalize on this by being extra helpful and immediately looking for a matching shirt and tie, for example. The same applies to the social chit-chat;

local gossip and football are popular topics. The fact that men buy clothing from a functional perspective is also evident from the fact that much of men's clothing is bought by their partners. It's a necessary evil, as they say. However, this is much less the case for young people. Young men (under 30) are more fashion conscious, more concerned with themselves and their appearance, and will therefore go shopping for nice clothes, often with their girlfriend.

RUNNING ON INTUITION, HOW FAST AND FOR HOW MUCH LONGER?

On 14 June I was getting dressed, full of good spirits, for a half marathon, when I noticed my running watch had stopped. Now you need to know that the Garmin Forerunner is little less than a minicomputer with navigation, heart rate monitor, speed and distance meter, as well as time keeping, so that was a bit of a shock. However, the organization usually has kilometres marked along the route and time clocks at fixed points (5, 10 and 15 km), so I would have some information at least. Just my luck, this organization did NOT have kilometre markers and the only clock was at the finish. So I had to run on intuition, for how long, where to, how far? You know nothing!

So there you are running, without knowing whether you've got another half hour or an hour to go, or whether you're running really fast or at your normal (!) pace. Whether you're almost there or still have a couple of kilometres to go. You're surrounded by runners with an iPod, so asking them is out of the question and after a while it makes no difference anyway, because you can't even talk any more, what a mess! In the end I ran 5 minutes slower than my normal time and I was a bit peeved until I realized that shopkeepers must feel the same. They know nothing about their customers; don't know who will come into the shop, when and why and whether they will buy anything. Everything's done on intuition. Web retailers, on the other hand, have all sorts of modern technology to help them, they know who's come in, when, how long they stayed and what they've looked at. Pity the shopkeeper, I thought to myself, who has to suffer the misery and uncertainty every day that I only experienced once during this half marathon.

Going shopping with friends is something women do more often than men; for many women it is a popular pastime, sometimes even an addiction: shopaholics. People go shopping to beat boredom, because it's enjoyable or because they want to treat themselves. The enjoyment element plays an important role and should be stimulated by the retailer. Many shops are set up to capitalize on the rational shopper: sale, clearance, discount! But do they meet the needs of the sociable shoppers? Does the retailer understand that these shoppers are looking for a kick, a surprise, a happy moment? If so, then they would surely giftwrap the purchases and give away a token surprise now and again! Shopping should be entertaining; customers should be left feeling happy when they make their purchase. It's precisely these surprising aspects that could make shopping fun for the hedonistic shopper, but little attention is being given to this as yet. In fact, the shops are focused on transactions and on the rational and functional shopper. The result is that hedonistic shoppers try their luck elsewhere, or spend their leisure time in a different way.

Hedonistic shoppers are seeking experiences. These experiences can include visiting different shops, trying on clothing, trying perfumes, but also secondary aspects such as how the shop is fitted, the look of the buildings or the sense of luxury and exclusivity. This can be seen in Harrods of London: the building looks very impressive, is in a top location close to Hyde Park and Kensington Gardens and the atmosphere is exclusive. The interior matches this image with a different ambience for each department and each section of the store. The Egyptian staircases are renowned and create a unique atmosphere and experience. It's only natural that customers come from all over the world to London to visit Harrods; you can buy anything and you feel special here. Not only are the articles luxurious and special, but the service is too. How would you like a personal shopper, an assistant who accompanies you throughout the shop so that you never have to look for anything and never have to carry anything? You can pay in one single transaction or have it put on your account. Your personal shopper also accompanies you to your car, or has the purchases delivered to your home, immediately if you wish.

We offer 100 per cent satisfaction or your money back – no questions asked.
Thank you for shopping at Harrods.

This text is found in various places in the Harrods department store in London. A sign of assurance, trust and hospitality.

This kind of service can also be found in other luxury stores such as Bloomingdale's or Saks Fifth Avenue. Even the locations of these stores, in Chicago and Manhattan, New York, are worth visiting. Shopping is a treat and all shops and all services join in. There is a Starbucks on every street corner!

In the centre of London alone there are 260 Starbucks cafés, a number which is planned to double over the next two years. Funshopping is a reaction to rational shopping.

For customers, buying is a secondary issue that just happens to you when you see something that you didn't even intend to buy, a real impulse buy, or something you buy to make yourself happy. The environment largely determines your mood and your inclination to buy. For hedonistic shoppers that is the decisive factor. This categorization, rational or hedonistic, is based on customer behaviour. This behaviour is actually seen in all customers and depends on the time (moment), type of item and environment. Even people who don't really like shopping can become inspired by the market stalls in their holiday destination or the purchase of a new car. It's a challenge to recognize this behaviour and to capitalize on it. It also has to be accepted that one can never please everyone, it's about pleasing the majority, but 'the majority' is made up of individuals who each have a good reason to buy. Quite what that reason is, is for the retailer to discover at the moment of contact.

Different kinds of products can also influence individual purchasing behaviour. A clear distinction can be made between shopping goods and convenience goods, but from an individual perspective. Groceries and no-nonsense items are categorized as convenience goods, while items with a high personal experience factor, and often a higher price label, are classified as shopping goods. However, this difference is not as sharp as is sometimes suggested. Especially in the case of convenience goods, personal elements such as available time, money and involvement with the product or the shop can be significant. This is especially noticeable in the purchasing behaviour of the better-off and the less well-off. Suddenly, goods that for the less well-off were previously shopping goods have become convenience goods. Shopping is then seen as a normal pastime and a fact of life.

The difference is also clearly visible during holidays, where there is a different buying pattern. During holidays in countries where prices can be haggled, time is a crucial factor. The buyer has less time but does have money and the vendor has lots of time and no money. The final price is agreed in a sort of trade-off between time and money. If you have enough time (and nerve) you can haggle the initial offer down considerably. In China it's even possible to negotiate the price down to 10–20 per cent of the initial offer, provided you take the time. The difference between shopping goods and convenience goods is therefore diffuse and determined by individual circumstances.

Additionally, there are also the impulse buys; unplanned, but bought anyway. This is because you see the item unexpectedly or experience some other trigger that makes you consider buying something. These are typical impulse buys that often make the customer feel good. This is taken into account in a good shop layout, but a good sales assistant will also point out an attractive tie, a ring or a handbag that would look good with the particular dress you are trying on. Impulse buys arise in part from an intrinsic emotion, a desire to have something, but can also be stimulated through personal contact or by seeing the item. On the Internet this is more difficult.

Negotiations on the price of items is part of the holiday fun. Nowadays the game is changed, no longer is it a matter of bargaining, but a matter of selling. The shopkeeper will just ask, after mentioning a price, 'You tell me what you want to pay.' The shopkeeper then decides if they want to sell. It takes the fun out of bargaining but it is fair. You pay the price you want to pay and the shopkeeper sells if a profit can be made.

The 'Shopping 3.0' Model

Shopping 1.0	Buying from local shops or craftsmen. Sometimes 'off the shelf', sometimes handmade.
Shopping 2.0	Non-store retailing. Mail order companies, door-to-door sales, coupons form an alternative to local shops and craftsmen. Practically only 'ready made' products are sold.
Shopping 3.0	Buyers are using all channels for information and shopping. Mostly information is first gathered from the Internet before checking in the store. A decision is made to buy online or in the store (cross-channel retailing based on buying behaviour).

Figure 2.1   The Shopping 3.0 model

The ORCA model is based on shopping 3.0 (Figure 2.1): first, search at home, then, check on the Internet in web-shops, next look in the real shop and, finally, decide where to buy!

A March 2010 study from the e-tailing group and PowerReviews found that one-half of Internet users carry out research online before making any type of purchase – on the Web, in a store or through any other method. They typically said that doing their own research online saved them time and made them more confident about their purchases.

Retailers' sites played an important role in the research process, and respondents said the most critical feature for a retailer to offer was product reviews by other customers. A lack of user-generated reviews would cause nearly one-half (49 per cent) of respondents to leave a retailer's site.

Though the '2010 Social Shopping Study' found that customer reviews had a strong influence on the purchases of 71 per cent of respondents – while only 25 per cent said the same about Facebook fan pages – an earlier e-tailing group study of Web merchants found that Facebook had caught on so strongly that more planned a presence on the social networking site in the next year than would have customer reviews.

It all starts at home when you realize that you need something; the problem recognition phase. You used to have to wait until you knew what you were going to buy, and you only did that in town. You'd go from shop to shop, collecting folders and talking with sales people. This was the orientation phase, which generally moved smoothly into the information phase. You then thought about it, discussed it with friends or your partner before you decided what you wanted to buy. Often, on Saturdays, the pavement cafés were filled with couples busy talking and trying to convince each other, while enjoying a cup of coffee. Usually some form of agreement would be reached after which the purchase would be made. Now, for most people, those days are a thing of the past. As soon as the orientation phase begins, the computer is booted up and you go looking for what you need. The initial screen is then important: Google, eBay or a web-shop, whatever your preference may be. You type in a search word, or a brand name, surfing from site to site and from page to page. It is often also possible to click on banners for extra information, and on hyperlinks to get more details or to order extra products. The customer thus surfs the net to come to a buying decision. Once they have got all the information and formed a clear preference for a particular product or a brand, the decision will be taken.

INTERNET SEARCHING FOR INFORMATION BEFORE MAKING A PURCHASE

Before Belgians make a purchase, they search the Internet for information to decide what they will buy where. In the case of ordinary products like clothing, 40 per cent search online for information before making a purchase. With cars the percentage of Belgians that first look for online information on the Internet can reach 83 per cent.

Source: www.publi4u.be/nl.

This decision may be taken at home, over a glass of wine. Often the purchaser's partner is consulted and a joint decision to buy the item is made. This is a purchase moment with a low buying threshold; you're sitting in your own home environment and can decide together with your partner or friends on the basis of all the information gathered. You know what is on sale and where you can buy it. All that's left is the question of where to actually buy it. There is a need, especially for the more expensive items, to see it, to feel it or even smell the product, and perhaps you want to take it with you right away. So then you go to the shop after all to evaluate your choice and to see the product. That is actually the moment of truth for a retailer, after all here's a customer with clear buying signs and a clear buying motive. Selling should actually be easy at this point, but it's not.

AMSTERDAM – In the Netherlands women make the most expensive purchases on the Internet, 7 per cent spend more than 2,500 Euros per year, while only 2 per cent of the men spend that much. Men indicate that they gather most of their information on the Internet (90 per cent), while 43 per cent of women find information in the traditional manner: by word of mouth. This was revealed in research by CheetahMail Nederland, conducted by Trendbox.

The survey showed that Dutch consumers prefer to find information through the Internet (85 per cent) and online newsletters (35 per cent) as opposed to the traditional channels like TV advertising (14 per cent) or newspaper advertisements (13 per cent). Four years ago newspapers were the most popular channel and only 15 per cent used the Internet.

Table 2.2   Differences between the classic buying process and new-style shopping

PHASE	PHYSICAL PROCESS	NEW-STYLE SHOPPING
Orientation	Talking with friends Looking in shops Newspaper advertisements Leaflets	Surfing on the Internet Checking out weblogs Discussing on social media like Hyves
Information	Advertisements on TV and radio Talking to sales staff	Newsletters Referrals on other sites
Buying decision	Asking specific questions of sales staff, viewing and trying product Catalogues, brochures and showrooms Often in the shop or the neighbourhood of the shop Sometimes at home evaluating with the brochures to hand	Weblogs, specific sites, comparison sites, users' experiences Product sites and web-shop sites for information At home on the basis of all the information At the computer screen
Purchase	In the shop of one's choice on the basis of personal preference and buying motives	Often directly from a web-shop, sometimes in the shop of one's choice, highly depends on personal preferences

Consumers between the ages of 16 and 24 are more open to e-mail offers (52 per cent) than the older generation (39 per cent).

Source: www.Nu.nl, 1 February 2006.

Suddenly entrepreneurs are dealing with mindful, well-informed customers. These customers also have the choice of where to buy and are not led by location or a smart sales talk. These customers know which questions to ask (and what answers to expect) and what a reasonable price would be. The customers that today's retailers are facing are also articulate, and that can be really difficult. This demands a lot of knowledge from the retailers, knowledge of buying processes, of products and of the buying motives. You need to be able to convince a customer to buy by using this knowledge, otherwise they will head off to their computer and buy the same product online for a lower price. Competition has become stiffer; the customer needs to be persuaded of the added value of shops and the advantage that they get from purchasing in shops. The price difference between shops and the Internet needs to be compensated.

There are only a couple of ways of doing that:

- By the shop itself: shopping nearby means not having to wait for your order, but being able to take the goods home straight away.

- Through the ambience in the shop, the service and the friendly contacts, through the convivial atmosphere, the surprise element (social aspects) and the enjoyment of placing the order for the purchase.

- Confidence in the product, the shop and the retailer. The latter is especially important. Exchange or money back – no questions asked, is the very least a shop can offer. Anything else, gift vouchers, credit notes or exchange with receipt, is a sign of mistrust towards the customer. They'll then go and buy from an Internet shop with a home shopping warranty mark, which allows you to send the product back with a money-back guarantee up to two weeks later (based upon proposed EU legislation).

- Through service, home delivery, even installation or taking away the old product. Followed up by, 'And if you still have any questions feel free to drop in.'

If the local shop is no longer able to offer an added value or if customers can't see why they should pay more for a product than on the Internet then the retailer has a problem. There has to be an added value from the customer's perspective. If that is missing a customer will be inclined to want to negotiate the price. The price on the product is then regarded as an opening bid by the retailer, open for discussion. If the retailer goes along with this, customers will become even more daring and regard it as logical to negotiate on the price. This is actually a sign that customers do not sufficiently recognize the added value or begrudge the shopkeeper their margin.

What Extra Effort are Retailers Currently Making?

My clothing store was not open to my suggestion that they should give me a discount on my new suit or give me either the shirt or the tie as a gift. But they did say: 'You don't buy a new suit every day, you should celebrate that. If we give you a bottle of champagne then you can celebrate buying your suit in style!' A positive approach that pleased me. Quite different to my shoe shop, where I had my Church shoes repaired, to the tune of 110 Euros. I still had to pay 3.50 Euros for the socks I bought at the same time. What a missed opportunity to please me. When I buy running shoes from my online running shop there is always a pair of running socks enclosed with my order as a service. Normally they're about 15 Euros. This also makes me feel happy!

In recent years it has become much easier to buy on the Internet, almost everything is for sale and can be found quickly. Of course, Google is a boon. About 70 per cent of buyers begin their search with Google or Yahoo or use Google during the information gathering phase. eBay is also used a lot, to see whether something is being offered for sale, or whether there is any more information there, and even new products are sought and bought on eBay. Finally there are the well-known and preferred web-shops. This means searching has become very diffuse and web retailers have to search for customers too. Where the purchase is ultimately made, be that on the Internet or in a real shop, is very much a personal choice and also depends on the product concerned. Software, books and music are easier to buy online than DIY items or home furnishings, for instance. The consumer also has confidence in the home shopping warranty mark. Some 70 per cent of customers stated that they prefer to shop at a web-shop that carries a guarantee, a very clear terms and condition agreement and a money back guarantee.

TRANSPARENCY ABOUT THE RETAILER YOU ARE PURCHASING FROM

- Statement of identity, 'Who we are';

- easy, direct and permanent access to company details of the terms and conditions;

- as clear and honest as possible.

RESOLUTION OF COMPLAINTS AND DISPUTES

- Clear information about how and where you can make a complaint;

- mediation of complaints and disputes;

- the handling of your complaint by an independent disputes commission.

CLEAR GUARANTEES AND TERMS AND CONDITIONS

- Clear information on after-sales service and commercial guarantees;

- clear information about the terms and conditions.

Other elements that contribute to trust are the number of payment methods offered, the possibility of paying afterwards (using a giro collection form) and also the possibility of paying by credit card or Paypal. A 'not satisfied', money back guarantee, like the one provided by a home shopping warranty mark, contributes to a large extent to online ordering. For websites, colour design, navigation and speed is a big advantage.

Webcams

Webcams have become standard components of notebooks and netbooks. It is simple to switch the cam on, so that the other person can watch what you are doing and you can watch them. Calls made through Skype are therefore extremely cheap (free, in fact), but are also really nice because you can see the other party. Webcams in shops are fun too, to be able to see how the shop looks, whether it's busy and even the opportunity to 'cam' with a manager for further advice. The webcam thus creates a bridge between the virtual experience and the physical experience. Through the webcam it seems as if you really do have physical contact.

In the buying process the webcam can add value through the personal support that can be given by a real person. The greatest restriction is that suppliers are still hesitant about offering this service as it means someone has to be present to hold the conversation. This is actually an unfounded anxiety: if the customer wants direct contact and to see the sales staff, thanks to the integration of a webcam in the laptop, the sales staff don't even need to be in the office or shop, they can be anywhere in the world and still have direct contact with customers. Customers will increasingly start to demand these sorts of contact, for customer services, after sales, and during the orientation and information phases. The integration of this technique immediately forms the bridge between physical shopping and virtual shopping.

Another improvement is the increasing speed of the Internet; shaky screen images are almost a thing of the past. The experience is becoming more and more realistic and the webcam is becoming an integral part of the shopping 3.0. Existing shops can now build this into their site, by placing a camera on the street and pointing it into the shop. This creates a bond for the customer; web retailers can use it for their customer contact. If customers really want this then retailers mustn't lag behind.

Routine Provides Structure and Reassurance

Suddenly the world is your oyster, you can buy wherever and whenever you want, there's no limit to the information you can access and lack of knowledge is a non-issue. It's an era of transparency, but also an era of searching. Always looking for special offers, for information and for the website you bought from the last time. Even on the Internet routine strikes! Worldwide there are now some 800 million active websites, but we have our preferences: 90 per cent of British people only view British websites (or English language websites). Immigrants will look at websites, and maybe also buy from web-shops, from their native country, although with the Internet it is not known if the shop really is in their native country or elsewhere. More and more English web-shops aim at immigrants by providing a specific look and feel to the site and specific products to remind them of home. It is thought that our activities remain restricted to approximately five sites, which we return to time and again. We have preferred destinations for finding out information: Google and Yahoo are favourites. Customers favour the well-known shops and the social networking sites such as Facebook and LinkedIn. There might be a few other sites in the each user's bookmarks, but that's about as far as it goes. Despite all the transparency, we search routinely and find security in the restriction! That's why we like buying from familiar sites, from well-known country-specific sites and from sites where we have had a positive experience. Amazon. co.uk carries the lowest risk, buying a book or DVD is not really the most challenging purchase. Because so many visitors trust Amazon the offering is no longer restricted to books and DVDs. More and more products, which are easy to buy and fun to use, are offered. From running shoes to toys, as long as it is easy to buy and adds fun to our lives, we will purchase it.

Therefore, more and more trust is built up in online buying. English language sites are our preferred locations, but once you have good experiences when using a foreign site, confidence can grow: first the English language version of the websites belonging to foreign web-shops and then sites in other languages. Comparisons are increasingly made between local sites and foreign sites. The prices of English language books are compared on Amazon.co.uk (or Amazon.com) or Barnes and Noble with Smith or A1books.com. For European customers, sites showing the prices in dollars and pounds were very popular at the beginning of 2009, the exchange rate for the euro was high and you could therefore buy relatively cheaply and easily from abroad via the Internet.

English sites also claimed a substantial growth in foreign visitors for electronic goods and clothing. Customers prefer to buy within the UK as the items purchased can be delivered to the home within a day or two and without customs duties. This notion is beginning to get through to customers, but not to web retailers as yet. Although they use email for making contact with their customers, seldom are local differences are used. Foreigners like to buy abroad when the price is lower and the service is good, but they like it even more if the communication is personal. Like a special offer for Dutch buyers or special promotions for the French on 14 July. The sales to foreigners (the few expats excluded) are still limited. However, changes can be seen on the 'information' sites: English people abroad are reading English newspapers via the Internet, buying from foreign websites is then only a small step away.

Foreigners Have a Different Culture

There's another important element that restricts this cross-border behaviour, and that is cultural differences. A foreign site looks different to an English site; you won't have a 'match' so quickly. It's still not enough to have a translation of the site to attract foreigners or to make purchases abroad. The look and feel of the site must also be right, as well as several small confidence-inducing details like payment methods, contact options (in own language) and a security feature like a home shopping warranty hallmark. Customers also choose certainty (trust and security) abroad. This is naturally much less the case for virtual products like software and news; these messages don't have that restriction because they are downloadable.

Different rules also apply for products that are not for sale in their own country. It is important for British people abroad to still be able to buy British products, the tie with the mother country remains strong. Enjoyable shopping has many dimensions, partly defined by what is available (locally), partly by the possibilities of mobility and technology, but to a large extent by customer demand: individual wishes, perhaps convenience, perhaps spoiling oneself and perhaps because there is a necessity. Enjoyable shopping can best be done in physical shops that are close to each other within an inspiring environment. The city or town centre used to be such an environment, but due to all sorts of restrictions it's increasingly becoming a shopping centre with entertainment facilities. Emotion will play an ever more important role on the Internet too. Videos on a website, short films, chat facilities and the integration of the webcam offer interaction and visual experience. This development is still in its infancy but, with this, Internet shopping will become a serious threat to funshopping.

Summary

- Enjoyable shopping starts at home. Make sure you can be found, with a high-hit entry on Google/Yahoo, with an entry on web-shops and in portals.

- Make the website attractive, renew the layout regularly (every three years at most, and post new messages at least once a week). Play around with the topics, news items and range on offer. Make sure you have attractive photos on the site and especially short film clips.

- Make sure you use direct communication, via email and also via the site (buying suggestions) and letters.

- Think from the customer's perspective and help the customer to buy. Integrate the Internet within the physical shop experience.

- Web retailers should offer service and fast delivery and they have to be innovative (webcams).

- Make shopping enjoyable, surprise your customers and use personal communication.

Online Shop Emancipation: A Fact in Ten Years' Time

Women have caught up with men in the last ten years when it comes to online shopping. Where nine out of ten online shoppers were men in 1998, now it's 51 per cent women. In the last ten years the number of people shopping online multiplied 40 times and online consumer spending grew more than 700 times faster than the total retail trade. This growth will continue and online shopping will evolve rapidly from functional to more of an experience.

There seems to be almost no difference any more between ordinary shopping and online shopping. The Internet used to be something that was mainly for men and for a functional evaluation aimed at the comparison of prices and specifications. In the last ten years online shopping has become more enjoyable, with consumer reviews and assessments and much more product and shop experience. That is something that also inspires women. In addition, it seems online shopping no longer has any disadvantages for the majority of people. Ten years ago people used to worry about the security of online payments and the reliability of delivery. To all intents and purposes this is a non-issue nowadays, with new methods like Paypal and a history of positive experiences.

The developments in relation to online shopping are marked in part by the fact that, since 1998, people have been spending a lot more time on the Internet. Nowadays 70 per cent of people (aged between 16 and 75) are online for more than six hours a week. For three out of four online shoppers (75 per cent) that is even more than 16 hours a week. Ten years ago that was just 15 per cent.[2]

Women

Women generally have different shopping behaviour to men. Women want, more than men, to find as much information as possible on products and prices and to be inspired; you see the same in traditional retail. Men want to be able to choose quickly. Web-shops are getting better at offering that combination. It's the shop experience that counts and brings customers in and keeps them. Book and music sites show exclusive previews of films, for instance, release the first chapters of new book titles, broadcast online from the North Sea Jazz Festival, and so on. YouTube got more than a billion visitors within two years

---

2   Blauw Research, 2009 on behalf of www.BOL.com.

showing short clips of people, and also products and education. Nowadays YouTube is an important search engine for product information and user experience.

From Functional to Experience

Along with better fulfilment of the functional needs of consumers – for example, with better product descriptions and illustrations, price comparisons, a large assortment, convenient ordering and delivery reliability – the web-shops are getting better, so it seems, at fulfilling the emotional shopping needs of the consumer by inspiring them more and more. Online shoppers can increasingly involve each other by sharing product experiences and exchanging quality assessments of the products on offer and the service provided – or not provided, as the case may be. Some web-shops feature user experiences in 'guestbooks'. Of course, most are positive and sometimes even names and email addresses are mentioned; in some cases there are even fan sites on social media like Facebook. Users of certain products or web-shops like to keep in touch and share their (positive) experiences.

A new development is the use of webcams, so the visitor can make face-to-face contact with the shop, and the use of video clips. Animations and video clips add to the buying experience and can be fun too. No longer is it sufficient to have a text-only website and even pictures won't generate any emotion. Text and pictures are only for rational sites; for rational shopping the fact that the websites are fast and simple to use is an advantage. Web-shops should be aware of why people visit the website and where they are accessing the Internet from. In the comfort of your own home you feel happy and this happy feeling should be projected on the website. Web retailers should make it easy to shop, give good product information, display their goods well (with clear photographs and descriptions) and provide the buyer with advice about the product, the delivery time and also about other products. Retailers should use historical data or data gathered through this navigation process. Customers appreciate suggestions for other product purchases and, if the combination makes sense, such as a shirt, tie and cufflinks, the customer is very likely to buy the combined offering. For example, Levi's has a 'friends' store linked to Facebook. Friends suggest articles to each other – a form of social shopping on the Internet.

BARRIERS TO CROSS-BORDER TRADE ARE HINDERING DEVELOPMENT

A new report on 'barriers to e-commerce' that will be presented by the European Union (EU) Commissioner for Consumer Protection Meglena Kuneva today shows that Internet shopping is gaining popularity in the EU, but it also warns that the barriers to cross-border trading are hindering its development. In the report published today a detailed analysis of the current trends in e-commerce in the EU are presented, including a breakdown per country, the most frequently purchased items and the barriers on the Internet for consumers and companies. The percentage of EU consumers that had bought at least one article through the Internet rose between 2006 and 2009 from 27 per cent to 33 per cent. These averages mask the immense popularity of Internet shopping in countries such as the United Kingdom, France and Germany, where more than 50 per cent of Internet users made an online purchase in the last year. In the Warranty Mark North-European countries (Denmark, Sweden, Norway, Finland and Iceland) 91 per cent of the Internet users bought products and services online in 2008. The market is also growing fast in countries like Italy and Spain. In contrast to this pattern of rapidly growing national markets the volume of cross-border online purchases is small at only 7 per cent in 2008 (in comparison to 6 per cent in 2006). In the report the many barriers, such as languages, regulations and practical issues, but also an important point such as trust, are said to be impeding the development of Internet shopping in the EU.

'Consumers have everything to gain with the Internet,' stated Commissioner Kuneva.

It offers access to a larger market with more suppliers and a greater choice. Thanks to the Internet, consumers can compare products, suppliers, and prices on an unprecedented scale. The use of the Internet for retail trade purchases will undoubtedly become a widespread practice. Already 150 million consumers shop online, but only 30 million of them indulge in cross-border online shopping. We must ensure that the development of e-commerce is not unnecessarily delayed because we are unable to remove important barriers of a regulatory nature or because important problems related to consumer confidence cannot be solved.

The Most Important Findings

1   E-COMMERCE IS GOING WELL

Consumers are generally satisfied with online shopping. On average, consumer satisfaction is higher than for the retail trade, especially relating to frequently bought products like computer-related purchases, but also to amusement and leisure items.

Consumers are especially satisfied with the comparison of prices, the larger range of goods on offer, the affordability of products and the choice of suppliers.

Consumers are less enthusiastic about matters such as clear product information, advertising, protection of privacy, trust and the ability to return goods.

2   CROSS-BORDER E-COMMERCE OFFERS CONSIDERABLE OPPORTUNITIES

One-third of EU citizens would consider purchasing a product or service from another member country through the Internet because it's cheaper or better.

One-third of EU consumers say that they are prepared to buy goods or services in another language. In a multicultural Europe there is a need for more options and a wider range of products than local shops or major brands can offer.

3   THE OPPORTUNITIES OFFERED BY CROSS-BORDER TRADE ARE NOT BEING REALIZED

The number of consumers in the EU that shop online rose between 2006 and 2008 from 27 per cent to 33 per cent, while the cross-border e-commerce remained the same. Only 7 per cent of consumers currently buy online abroad and the gap is increasing rather than decreasing.[3]

The Most Important Barriers

1.   Geographic fragmentation: these days most traders have a website that can be viewed by consumers everywhere. Yet most retailers still seem to work on the assumption that the internal market is divided up per country. There is a whole range of possibilities but, in practice, it comes down to consumers being refused a purchase or being referred back to their own country.

---

3   The European Commission, 2009.

Practical and regulatory barriers, including:

1.   Barriers in terms of language continue to be a problem for most traders and consumers, although we mustn't exaggerate its importance. Indeed, 60 per cent of all retailers are already prepared for transactions in more than one language.

2.   Logistics problems with respect to the interoperability of post and payment systems and issues relating to access to broadband links.

3.   Barriers of a regulatory nature seem increasingly unjustified for consumers and companies; for example consumer law, VAT rules, regulations about selective distribution, protection of intellectual properties, the transformation of EU legislation on waste processing into national legislation.

4.   Barriers that undermine consumer confidence mainly concern unwillingness in matters relating to payments, deliveries, complaints, application of guarantee terms and conditions, requests for repayment (customer services), as well as privacy issues. Any difficulties are experienced as worse with cross-border transactions.

Source: European Commission, March 2009.

3

Shopping Evolution: How to Adapt to Survive

Charles Darwin (1809–1882), renowned for his theory of evolution: life is evolving, plants and animals adapt to survive.

Adam Smith (1723–1790), philosopher and economist, famed for his views on economics: specialization leads to higher productivity and little government interference. An invisible hand steers the economic processes.

Life is evolving – that is true for mankind, the business community and nature. There is a past, a present and a future. But what are the developments, and what are the causes of change? I can imagine that this occupied Darwin when (as a geologist) he started examining the evolution of the Earth and also studied environmental developments. The turbulent changes following the Industrial Revolution a hundred years earlier also inspired him to place developments in a time context. Could there be a natural evolution in the environment as there is in the economy? Are developments not derived from each other and related to each other? This was a challenge for Darwin, but this challenge still exists today for policy makers, entrepreneurs, physicists and, for example, economists. As is examined in this book, the changes arising from the use of the Internet lead to adaptations in customer buying behaviour, which in turn must lead directly to changes in marketing, organizations and retail. Are there analogue developments and learning experiences? The past is, after all, also the basis for the future.

Would Charles Darwin also have wondered all this when he set out on his now legendary voyage on HMS Beagle? The voyage lasted from 1831 to 1836 and took him to many, very distant parts of the world, such as South America, Australia and New Zealand. The Galapagos Islands, in particular, made a deep impression on Darwin. The voyage began in the expectation that Darwin, as a physicist and geologist, would conduct research that would lead to a theory contradicting any notion of evolution of the earth or of life and nature on earth. Religious fundamentalists in Europe distanced themselves strongly from the new insights that were beginning to develop among scientists with regard to the beginning of life on Earth.

It all turned out quite differently. In his search for the development of life on Earth, he became inspired by Charles Lyell, who referred to the formation of the earth as an evolutionary process. In 1835, Darwin landed on the Galapagos Islands off the coast of Ecuador and became familiar with various endemic animal species (which only occur in one place) and the mutation of birds and other animals which differed from island to island. He also noticed that these animals were not afraid of human beings. The islands were of volcanic origin and were, in most instances, sparsely vegetated. Survival for people was difficult if not impossible. Each island had been formed at a different time, through volcanic eruptions, and the development on each island, and the survival conditions for its creatures, also differed. In order to survive the animals therefore had to mutate. These animals had no natural enemies; where would they come from on a new island in the middle of the ocean?

The various types of animals, and later plants, had appeared on the islands by chance. Winds from a particular direction had carried the seeds as well as certain birds; ocean currents had brought the fish and penguins, for example. In this way a new, untouched natural environment formed in complete ecological harmony. Animals and plants were able to develop for centuries without any natural enemies. The cactuses have no spines and animals build their nests wherever they want. Even now they still have the sense that nothing can harm them (the Galapagos Islands are a protected area).

His experiences during this sea voyage inspired Darwin to develop his theory of evolution, based on species that could evolve in different forms. Various scientific publications supported his theory. Other scientists came to the same conclusion; life on Earth is subject to evolution. *It's not the largest or the strongest that survive, but those that can adapt the best.* His theory of natural selection met a lot of opposition, especially his notion that this also applied to humans and that our species could be ape-like. Churches and believers considered this blasphemy. For the evolution of plants and animals, however, there was more understanding. His research and his many scientific publications eventually led to the book *The Origin of Species*[1] (1859), a sizeable volume (almost 500 pages) which is a good reflection of his views and those of fellow scientists. It is an analysis that is still impressive and, although our knowledge now extends much further and most of the conclusions have been revised, it still gives a good impression of the basis of life and the development of it through external circumstances. But what is true of the environment can also apply to other developments, where external circumstances can give rise to adaptations.

From Nature to Economics, From Darwin to Smith

The comparison between Charles Darwin and Adam Smith has often been made: could economics perhaps also be an evolutionary process? Is Adam Smith's invisible hand not the same as the hand of God? Comparison is difficult, the notion nevertheless inspiring; they are analogue developments, after all. Organizations also have to deal with changing external circumstances and are constantly wondering what the best strategy would be. Independent bodies that can mutate (change) are always making conscious or unconscious choices to be able to respond to changed conditions; people, animals and plants, but also organizations, governments, politics and other forms of collaboration. It is then also interesting to take the theory of evolution as the basis for the analysis of survival chances for organizations. Perhaps the same conditions apply and the circumstances in old markets perhaps differ from those in new markets, and are different for new products compared with those for old products. Can the Internet be regarded as a new market with new threats and new chances? Do the same opportunities and threats apply on the Internet as in the real, old world? The control of the old world is in the hands of established processes and structures that are embedded in the system and have thus applied for years. It seems as if an invisible hand is guiding this process towards a wider goal.[2] Economists later projected this invisible hand onto economic processes, on the conduct of those offering goods and services and consumer buying behaviour. Here, too, the economic principle applies in which consumers purchase in a rational manner and

---

1   Darwin, Charles, *The Origin of Species*, Random House Value Publishing Inc., London, 1979.
2   As described by Adam Smith in his book *Enquiry and Causes of the Wealth of Nations*, first published in 1776, Random House edition published 1994, page 485 (Book 4). The original publication was intented to minimalize the expenditure and activities of the Government. He also strongly advised specialization: 'A master will never make at home what it will cost him more to make than to buy.'

strive to attain maximum satisfaction of needs (the laws of Gossen[3]). This is described by Adam Smith in his book *An Inquiry into the Nature and Causes of the Wealth of Nations,* which was first published in 1776. In the Random House publication this appears on page 485 (Book 4). His original publication was aimed at minimizing government spending and intervention. He also pleaded for specialization: 'A master will never make at home what it will cost him more to make than to buy.'

It is, perhaps, not by chance that Adam Smith, a Scot, experienced the Industrial Revolution and all the developments that followed at close hand. He was confronted with huge changes, both industrial and societal. These changes inspired him to study the societal changes and industrial developments which eventually resulted in his book. In this tome (1131 pages) he discussed in great detail the changes in production, the role of the government and the consequences of both. Adam Smith is regarded as the founder of modern economics.

The broad interpretation of the invisible hand can be guiding for the current dynamics in markets and the natural buying behaviour of consumers:

> *The theory of the Invisible Hand states that if each consumer is allowed to choose freely what to buy and each producer is allowed to choose freely what to sell and how to produce it, the market will settle on a product distribution and prices that are beneficial to all the individual members of a community, and hence to the community as a whole. The reason for this is that greed will drive actors to beneficial behaviour. Efficient methods of production will be adopted in order to maximize profits. Low prices will be charged in order to undercut competitors. Investors will invest in those industries that are most urgently needed to maximize returns, and withdraw capital from those that are less efficient in creating value. Students will be guided to prepare for the most needed (and therefore most remunerative) careers. And all these effects will take place dynamically and automatically.*

---

3   Scarcity is the fundamental economic problem of having seemingly unlimited human needs and wants, in a world of limited resources. It states that society has insufficient productive resources to fulfil all human wants and needs. Alternatively, scarcity implies that not all of society's goals can be pursued at the same time; trade-offs are made of one good against others. Gossen's laws indicate that humans will try to buy as many articles as possible and make trade-off between one and another.

Entrepreneurship

'Survival, adaptation, seizing opportunities' are core words for an entrepreneur – this is followed by a dynamic process of adaptation, structuring and optimization. Until recently the trigger for a modification of such processes was specifically the goods or services that were on offer. Product changes, technological applications and changes in what was offered created a consumer demand that was to guide the modifications. Suppliers therefore sought opportunities in the market and studied consumer behaviour in order to discover where possibilities lay and what competitors were offering so that, with this knowledge, they could offer the market a non-standard proposition (competitive strategies).

The supply conditioned the process; the invisible hand in this consisted of reactions from the market, from customers, competitors and other relevant parties. The trigger was the modified supply that responded to a supposed demand, or to a latent desire. With Darwin the external conditions were a fact. These did not change and if the plants and animals wanted to survive then adaptation was the only option. In the current circumstances it's much more difficult for suppliers to condition the processes and the demand. Just as the plants adapted to the ecological conditions, the animals to the food supply, and they mutated to survive, so organizations will have to focus on the demand from consumers (or purchasing companies) in order to survive.

The supply has become transparent, fully surveyable and comparable for consumers and companies alike. On the Internet all sorts of information is just a click away. The market is no longer locally or regionally restricted, but actually nationwide and often even global. The supply is also easily comparable, so that consumers can make a choice on the basis of their own criteria. The changes in consumer demand have become the triggers for the supply and are driving the changes in markets and supply. Organizations will have to adapt to these changes. Consumers are no longer limited in their choice by the local supply.

This means Adam Smith's vision of the invisible hand is indeed applicable: freedom of choice leads to freedom of what to sell and to produce. As such, efficiency in the supply is achieved through greed or, in the current context, by profit goals and the urge to survive. In contrast to the past, however, it's no longer the supply that is scarce, it's the demand. Now that consumers have insight into the entire market (via the Internet and the use of search engines like Google) they can buy whatever they want, wherever they want. So now it's actually the supplier that has to adapt to the demand, to the customer and to the customer's buying process. This is a shift from a supply paradox, in which every supply will create its own demand, to a demand paradox, in which every demand can find a supply. In marketing terminology you could also say 'from persuasion (supply) to temptation (demand)'.

Evaluation or Evolution?

Darwin developed his theory of evolution in the first half of the nineteenth century. The second half of the eighteenth and the first half of the nineteenth century were a cradle for change and the basis for the current developments. It was a time when people contemplated life and major changes were brought about by inventions, by forms of collaboration and by the development of new technologies (the Industrial Revolution and its consequences). The UK achieved the status of a world power and was the inspirer of change. A different kind of world order evolved as well as other skills and competences. People had to adapt to survive, organizations were formed that could exercise power and competitive strengths were also defined at national level with the UK as the leading nation.

That was the picture of the world in which Darwin lived and conducted his research. However, his theory was applied to nature; economics was still regarded as a branch of philosophy and not a separate discipline. Adam Smith was a philosopher who, at the end of the eighteenth century, saw the impacts of the Industrial Revolution and studied the consequences of this and how the government should be responding. He is also regarded as the first (political) economist. Smith examined the changes, how they could be steered and what the consequences could be. He wanted the government to have a limited role and his vision of labour was one of productivity: the best productivity was achieved by specialization of labour. By testing the theory of evolution and likewise the vision of the invisible hand against current circumstances, a survival strategy can perhaps be deduced. Entrepreneurs nowadays have many questions for which answers are sought: how can shops survive the current changes? What is the right strategy with respect to the Internet and how do you respond effectively to customer behaviour? Do you still have to adapt in order to survive or do you just have to stay yourself? Do small companies and shops still have a chance or is it the large, strong companies that will survive? What is the value of marketing if it's so difficult to reach customers? The final question is naturally whether adaptation is sufficient or whether an organization actually has to change quite dramatically? Evaluation or evolution; that is the key question!

Adapt or Change

Right now, in the middle of the recession, organizations are fighting over the customer, the turnover and maintaining a decent profit. Entrepreneurs and managers are once again closely scrutinizing costs. This is not really revolutionary, more a question of slimming down and making an organization more efficient. The need to do this is not present in a growing market and when turnover is increasing. The need arises when there is contraction, low sales or a waning demand. Organizations then have to consider what is really needed to survive. People do this every day in the poor regions of Africa, but also in prosperous Europe. Keeping a hand on the purse strings is a reaction to a (presumed) shortage. Eating less is a reaction to less income or a desire to lose weight.

This is equally true for an organization; saving costs is a reaction to supposed loss of results or a wish to be more flexible. Despite the relevance of these savings in order to maintain profitability, it is not a real change. It's a form of downsizing: continuing to do the same, only on a smaller scale or with fewer costs – slimming down in other words. Real changes are not the result of a temporary shortage (conjunctural) but a consequence of a constant shortage or change (structural). During drought periods animals can manage very well with less water or even less food, but they still go looking for it.

This is also the right attitude for organizations; they can make changes not only through economizing, but also by responding to external circumstances, by going looking for water and food, that is, by approaching other markets or customers. After all, you could try eating different food if that means you can survive, therefore a company can offer other products and services, change the business model or serve customers in a different way. Organizations can deliberate about the degree of profitability, concentrate on profitable products or look at what profit opportunities there are. They therefore resemble people and animals, while the economic conditions have a lot in common with ecological conditions.

What Can You Do?

The question is whether to evaluate or evolve, to slim down or change – a fundamental question for everyone facing a change in circumstances. Good evaluation enables you to ascertain which are the good actions and the bad actions. On the basis of a SWOT (strengths, weakness, opportunities and threats) analysis, you will immediately know what your strengths for survival are and where your weaknesses lie. These weaknesses must make you stronger; otherwise the competition will use them to settle the score. What this in fact means is that customers are so averse to them that they no longer want to buy from you. These strengths and weaknesses can also be split into the factors through which they have arisen; external circumstances (the so-called exogenous factors) and the internal circumstances determined by the branch or product. There are also circumstances that lie within the sphere of influence of the entrepreneur – the endogenous factors. Such factors include location, personnel, assortment, service and price level (Table 3.1).

Table 3.1   Exogenous and endogenous factors influencing an organization

	ENDOGENOUSLY DETERMINED	**EXOGENOUSLY DETERMINED**
Endogenous factors	Culture	Use of technology
	Profit level	Customer orientation
	Organization form	Opening hours
	Decision making	Direct communications
	Price setting	
	Human resource management	
Exogenous factors	Price agreements	State-of-the-art technology
	Cartels	Competition
	Collaboration	Government policy
	Supply chain	Purchasing power
	Consumer organizations	International developments
		Buying process
		Buying motives

The table shows the relation between endogenous and exogenous factors that influence the goods and services offered by organizations. Endogenous factors that are defined within the sphere of influence of an organization, and exogenous factors that are influenced by external circumstances demand a strategic choice (horizontal axis). Exogenous factors that are determined exogenously are independent developments on which a business can exercise no influence. Exogenous factors that are endogenously determined arise from relations between parties in which an organization can participate.

Through evaluations, the endogenous factors can be assessed in terms of their value and it can be determined whether these would perhaps be improved by modifications. This is a process that every entrepreneur has to go through constantly. Look at your own actions and ask yourself: why are customers buying from *me*? What are we doing well and what are *we* doing poorly? This must not be viewed through the eyes of the entrepreneur, because they're usually focused on numbers (spreadsheets as the basis for decisions), but through the eyes of the customer or the potential customer, who consider relative differences: the differences between the various shops or suppliers they can choose from.

What Should Organizations do According to Darwin?

> *The amount of food available for each animal determines its ultimate size, but it is usually not food that determines the size but the attractiveness to other animals.*[4]

That also applies to organizations; the ultimate purchasing power demand defines how big a business can become and what turnover can be achieved (exogenously determined). To a large extent, the internal organization defines the maximum profit possible (cost structure and price level). This is a rigid approach which is applied in a supply-dominated market. The demand was always growing and new markets could be conquered. Market leaders in growth markets are always trying to achieve more growth and higher profits. A balanced competitive strategy, a well-chosen offer of goods or services and good target group communications were enough to make the company grow and flourish.

---

4   Page 120, *The Origin of Species.*

However, target groups are objectively defined groups of people, defined according to age, gender and place of residence, for example. People are individuals with their own wishes and preferences, who suddenly change their buying habits, find their information differently – subjectively and defined by the moment. It is therefore the attractiveness of the goods and services offered and the options available to customers that will determine what organizations can still sell. Customers choose the products they find the most attractive from what's on offer. Businesses therefore have to pay much more attention to the attractiveness of what they are offering on the basis of the customers' options. It is thanks to the Internet, and also to mobility, that the options open to customers have increased tremendously in recent years. As a supplier, how can you still get yourself noticed and what will make customers choose *your* product? This customer choice process is an exogenous variable that you can only influence to a limited extent. However, understanding this process will enable you to adapt the products and services you offer and modify your organization accordingly (flexibility). Slimming down may be a possibility if the price or flexibility influences a customer's decision-making process, but the service, provision of information and opening hours are often much more relevant.

Consequently, slimming down an organization is not the correct model because, in fact, everything remains the same, only the costs are lower. Companies need to change on the basis of the exogenous variables: the buying process and the customers' decision-making criteria. At times when the market is no longer growing, during a recession, you can still grow your business by increasing the attractiveness: attractiveness in the eyes of the customer, but also by becoming more attractive compared with other suppliers. This is a good strategy, especially when demand is waning. From this a lasting advantage can be built up that will continue to apply when the demand starts growing again. It's a shame that in times like that attention is only paid to economizing and not to making the products or the act of shopping more attractive, because that is what attracts customers and customer loyalty.

> *With plants and flowers that actually focus on the insects that come to them, there is a greater distribution of their seeds and pollens.*[5]

Sometimes organizations have to expend a lot of effort to acquire a customer, but are these then the most loyal of customers? The customers that have been difficult to acquire are often not the most profitable of customers and often remain highly critical. If a customer approaches an organization

---

5   Page 140, *The Origin of Species.*

spontaneously there is a high degree of affinity. Treated appropriately, these customers will later turn out to be very loyal customers. The Internet in particular offers the possibility of spontaneous customer acquisition; they visit your website and approach you or buy from your company. All a company has to do at this point is meet these customers' wishes and perhaps even surpass them.

What is striking about well-known, successful Internet entrepreneurs is the extent to which they are on the same wavelength as their customers; they belong to the very target group they are looking to reach with their website. They can sense precisely what the customers want. This is also very evident in their weblogs and also in the e-mails they receive from satisfied and surprised customers. This initiates a process of customers acting as ambassadors of the shops for other customers. In the past this was a deliberate strategy of companies (member-get-member) for which customers were rewarded. Anyone who introduced a new customer to the business was rewarded for this, in the form of a bottle of wine or a discount, for example. Customers will recommend web-shops even without a reward; it is now a spontaneous process that takes place outside the shop. If customers are satisfied they let this be known via weblogs, Twitter or e-mails. They like telling others about it.

In the old (supply-driven) world the market was not transparent to the customer and potential buyers had to be pointed towards a shop or product. Having a motivation to go shopping was important. This motivation consisted of a special offer, or an introductory discount – a recommendation by an acquaintance helped too! Nowadays the market is transparent, only customers often don't know what can be bought where. Recommendations from friends, acquaintances and even total strangers can help in this respect. A site, the online shop, has to be found. Then you find yourself on an unknown site wondering how to establish its reliability, and that of the products and the services offered. A good way of doing this is a weblog in which customers can give their opinions, preferably with name and e-mail address to ensure it's genuine and not rigged. Visitors will consequently gain confidence in the site, and in the supplier, and will also be more inclined to make a purchase. If these customers are satisfied they will be happy to share this with others. It is this voluntary choice, the voluntary bond, that ensures that buyers tell others about their good fortune. They become fans of the shop. They may also show this on social networking sites like Facebook, where shops also have 'friends' pages.

Larger species become even larger and will break up into smaller units and thus become even more dominant and provide dominant offspring.[6]

In recent decades, organizations grew fast, the market expanded and welfare increased. Each year, growth plans were made and a business plan with a reducing turnover or falling profits would not be accepted by management. Progress had to be made. In particular, large companies wanted to become even bigger, through autonomous growth, but that often took too long, so takeovers were needed. This process is typical of recent decades, and is also characteristic of the good times of the supply economy.[7]

Larger organizations were able to purchase better and more cheaply and were stronger in the competitive battle. Through size a position of power was also built up. More money could also be spent on marketing and, within that, on advertising. It was only logical that these organizations could attract ever-increasing numbers of customers. However, it was a power struggle within the context of the supply economy. Large companies may have difficulty in reaching their target markets if speedy actions are required. Under stable market conditions (stable exogenous variables) growth is possible by making progressively better use of production factors (resources) and an ever-better marketing approach. A strong position of power can be built up, market leadership can be attained, which can lead to greater customer loyalty and better purchasing conditions. In fact the organization can be large and dominant in the production and marketing chain and dominant in relationships (purchasing relationship and selling relationship).

These kinds of businesses are keen negotiators and attract loyalty from both suppliers and customers through their position of power. But clear organizational structures, rigid reporting procedures and long decision-making procedures are part and parcel of these companies.[8] There are also stakeholders

---

6   Page 113, *The Origin of Species*.
7   Supply economics is the study that deals with the effective use of production factors, including labour. Adam Smith is regarded as one of the first supply economists. Keynes, on the other hand, wished to know nothing about the supply economist who regarded freedom of commerce as important and who wished little government intervention (the invisible hand). He was a demand economist, who in fact wished to stimulate demand. In the context of this book, supply economics is regarded as the supply paradigm in which supply is leading the demand (this is also the basic principle of classic marketing) while it is now the demand that is leading the supply and the manner in which customers buy, a choice of channel, and unlimited freedom of choice for customers.
8   Managers also complain from time to time about the amount of time that has to be spent on reporting, especially in large stock exchange-listed enterprises. Decisions are made on the basis

who strive to achieve their own interests: profit interests, share prices that have to rise or other power-based interests.

CONTINUE TO ADOPT SOCIAL STRATEGIES

Next year promises to advance the consumer's desire to share information, as social strategies are rapidly evolving. 'Facebook, Twitter, and features such as forward to a friend, share with your network, consumer ratings and reviews, blogging, and microsite marketing will continue to be effective social strategies that retailers should adopt,' Marinelli states. Multichannel retailers need to have the agility to adapt to social strategies when they change and follow the consumers to the next opportunity. 'There are retailers out there who are trying to determine how to deal with social networking tools,' says Cannon. 'These retailers need to work social strategies in a way that's not just advertising their goods, but also allowing the customer to experience something more, such as providing assurance of seamless integration among their channels.' The lack of a coherent multichannel strategy, or one with unclear objectives, can hurt your revenue in 2010. Pay attention to multichannel retailing trends to gain a solid understanding of who your consumers are and what they want. Retailers that do so will find that they've added value to their organization and their customer's multichannel shopping experience.

Source: www.retailsolutionsonline.com, November 2009.

As soon as market conditions change or exogenous variables change, these organizations encounter problems. The power game is no longer working and slow decision making is seen as a major problem.[9] The first reaction is to 'keep doing the same but cheaper'. Suppliers are pressured into cutting their prices, creditor payment terms are extended whilst the debtors have to pay sooner, in cash if possible. Staff are asked to make sacrifices and the headcount is scaled down or frozen. Companies want to downsize but to carry on as before; keep growing and making profits. Ultimately, the company will be unsuccessful in this endeavour. The exogenous factors have not changed temporarily; they are

---

of spreadsheets; spreadsheet management is a much-heard complaint. Accountants also warn about the spreadsheet dictatorship. Spreadsheets seem simple but are often an obscure body of complex, interrelated formulae from which no one becomes any the wiser. The results are, however, regarded as absolute and not open to discussion. The basis for decision making is therefore not sound and a false reality is the consequence.

9   See, for example, the book *The Third Wave* by Alvin Tofler (1980), Bantam Books, on modifications of organizations.

permanently different. Customers also buy in a permanently (fundamentally) different way.

An additional problem is that the changing market conditions – which should ideally lead to a change in the control and form of the organization – have to be handled by the existing management. These management board members have experience of dealing with the supply paradigm and growth scenarios but they are unable to deal with a demand paradigm and diminishing turnover and profits, As a consequence, the decision making by these management teams is, at least, delayed. This delay leads to a diminishing of the adroitness of organizations (customers turn away and choose a different supplier) and also opens up opportunities for newcomers or competitors. Organizations now have to do something different and will thus choose to start up specialist units.[10]

Specialization, as Adam Smith called it, was based on labour but can be reflected in organizations. Small adroit units are more capable of responding to the change in demand and can maintain a better relationship with the increasingly diverse customers. This is precisely what Quinn also described in his 'competing values model'.[11] Organizations are still struggling with comparisons between flexibility and control: flexibility at the expense of control and vice versa.

In large organizations, it is specifically the control processes that are well under control, managing a large company would otherwise not be possible. In small organizations, which are often still headed up by the entrepreneur who started the business, the opposite is true: flexibility defines the strength of the company. This is at the expense of the control – processes are not functioning properly, reporting and reports are limited – however, members of staff have a high degree of autonomy and the entrepreneur reacts rapidly.

Small, flexible organizations or organizational units are consequently better able to deal with dynamic and rapidly changing market conditions. Remaining associated with a larger entity, a collaborative venture or a parent company will, however, increase the dominance of the collaboration (as in franchise chains) or the parent company. More and more organizations are therefore seeking a balance between flexibility and control. This can lead to new organizational forms. Additionally, there is a force field between internal orientation and external orientation.

---

10   See Quinn (1992); competing value model.
11   See Appendix 1.

In stable markets, and commonly in large organizations, there will be an internal orientation. It is important to have all processes in order, an efficient operational management and good reporting. Control and internal orientation go well together, as do flexibility and external orientation. Small organizations are good at external orientation linked to flexibility – they have short decision-making lines – while in large organizations, the many interests, stakeholders and power structures mean that internal orientation usually goes hand in hand with control. The shift in how businesses are steered lies mainly in responding to the changes in the market. These could be different competitive relationships but also actually other buying motives and processes. The Internet is an important catalyst of change and organizations have to consider this.

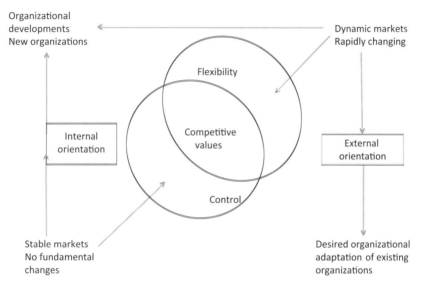

Figure 3.1   Quinn's Competing Values model

On the basis of Quinn's Competing Values model[12] (see Figure 3.1 and Appendix 1), the changing market conditions are determining the strategy to be followed. If a market is stable then a strong focus on (cost) control and a strong internal orientation, with a focus on efficiency, can be the right strategy. However, as soon as the market conditions change, as we see now with the recession and a change in buying behaviour, the organization also has to adapt. An external orientation is necessary to know what's happening in the

---

12 Competing Values model: in stable markets the focus will be on control and internal processes. In dynamic markets the focus will be on flexibility and a strong external orientation. For existing organizations it is important to be more flexible, new organizations faced with strong growth should focus more on internal processes and control.

market and why it's happening. In addition, businesses also have to consider what the consequences of this may be. The developments are never restricted to a particular function or a particular area but strongly influence each other, not least through the transparency of information and the direct forms of communication that are now possible through the Internet.

The organization has to change. That's easy to say, of course, but not always as easy to implement. All processes and structures are based on control, the 'drivers' of an organization are determined on the basis of the internal orientation, but reporting is also based on this. Many organizations are not used to change and the steering mechanisms are rarely defined on the basis of external factors. After all, the management has been trained to control, to manage, not to be entrepreneurs.

Some older managers, many of whom are started their careers in the boom time of the 1960s, have only known good times and are used to working in organizations that have grown and flourished, with a focus on control. That makes the transformation to a flexible, externally oriented company even more difficult. What is really needed is a totally new management that has external orientation, that doesn't sit in meetings all day, and that can direct a flexible organization and dynamic processes and structures. However, these leaders also have to contend with fixed patterns, with an existing culture and with employees who are used to set methods and procedures. A transformation is necessary but that can only happen if there's a sense of urgency.

The recession will therefore also be the start of other organizational forms and a modification of the structure of the company: more externally focused orientation, more flexibility, and a management that is more in touch with people and that has close contact with the customers. However, it must also be a management that can listen and allows staff to have their say. An organization's decision to split up into small independent units with several leaders and an external focus on small groups of customers is, therefore, a logical choice.

For a company starting up, the transformation process is precisely the opposite. The entrepreneur is driven by the opportunities that a market offers and can respond flexibly to market developments. However, as the organization grows it becomes increasingly difficult to be only flexible, processes also have to be controlled and quality has to be maintained, whilst financiers often become involved – demanding return on investments. These companies now have to improve process control, make the reporting uniform and make the organization independent of its founder. This is often a hard call, and Internet companies frequently go under because of their own success. The company grows so fast that there is suddenly a need for finance, and for additional overheads (such as websites, e-commerce platforms and IT infrastructure), and the founder can no longer oversee everything. There is also a high risk of illness or burnout. Securing knowledge and flexibility in systems is a sensible approach. The challenge is real, with the danger that it will still not succeed.

Both types of organization, small and large, must, as a result of the new market conditions, transform into businesses that are in touch with their customers, which are flexible yet also able to meet current operating requirements such as profitability. The current developments nevertheless lead to new opportunities for small organizations. Service and commitment are important mainstays, especially in the retail sector. Customers want access to small, local shops so as to avoid the hustle and bustle of a shopping centre.

There is currently a movement towards the small local shop, especially in the UK. The UK is traditionally a nation of shopkeepers of course; customers are used to the corner shop. However, these have almost disappeared as a result of the developments seen in recent decades. The overwhelming size of the shopping centres and the impersonal nature of the Internet have led once again to a growth of, and a customer preference for, smaller shops. The fact that they charge slightly higher prices is not important. The local facility, close to home, is becoming important again. The small independent shopkeeper is being replaced by small shops that collaborate with or are part of a larger concern.

Changes from a Historic Perspective

Changes can be viewed within an evolutionary context. We have seen that in modern times one change influences another, not merely consecutively but also simultaneously. Developments in one branch, country or function have immediate consequences for other branches, countries or functions. In this context, it is logical that organizations adapt to social and technological developments. The Industrial Revolution, in which Adam Smith found the inspiration for his vision of state intervention and labour (specialization), also had consequences for social relationships (a new industrial class and a workers' class) and for technology (efficient production methods). This ultimately led to extensive industrialization and the application of production technology. The film *Modern Times* (1936) demonstrates the consequences of this very well – Charlie Chaplin plays a factory worker who has become part of the machine.

Henry Ford was a proponent of efficient production. He wanted uniformity in output, efficiency and mass production and provided a definitive step from craft production to mass production; from hand-made to mass production. However, mass production is also linked to mass consumption and thereby also to how we work, how we buy and what we buy.

> *Flexible production dramatically reduced the demand for unskilled labour. Flexible production requires numerate and literate workers, capable of a high degree of self-direction. As a consequence, the number of unskilled industrial workers in the developed world has been falling for nearly 30 years. Decreased numbers have been reflected in political decline, as unskilled labour lost its leading role in the union movement and union influence in general has waned, and also in falling relative or, in some cases, real wages. Increasingly, workers are forced to choose between full employment (the US choice) and job security (Western Europe's choice).*

Source: Wikipedia on post-Fordism.

This was, in fact, a fundamental switch that formed the basis of the developments of the twentieth century. Some economists even talk of the before-Ford and after-Ford eras – BF and AF – or pre-Fordism and post-Fordism. The period from 1920–1940 is called pre-Fordism. The period from 1940–1960 was the period of massification, Fordism at its best, which (certainly in the USA) was typical of mass production and mass consumption. Next came the post-Fordism period, from 1960–1990, during which efficient production methods were linked to automation.

Mechanization became computerization – resulting in the supply economy – in which the supply was the leading factor, at the expense of unskilled labour. The rise of advertising, and later also marketing, was the result – the mass-produced articles had to be sold, after all. It also characterized another change: the creation of a generic demand and direct availability of the products. All products were comparable (mass production), made for an average demand, and suppliable from stock. The consumer no longer had to wait for the product to be made by the craftsman. The rise of marketing was inevitable to facilitate the volume of sales that had to be made. The demand economy (unit production and customized work) became a supply economy, based on mass volume, uniform wishes of the target group and fixed prices. This meant that consumption became important, consumptionism was fed by the rich supply, the tempting advertising and improved lifestyles.

Moreover, mass production's decline has been accompanied by a decline in mass consumption. Instead of standardized products designed and manufactured for the lowest common denominator, final products reflect the full array of preferences and pocketbooks. This too has probably exacerbated the trend to further real income inequality.

Source: Wikipedia on post-Fordism.

The period up to 1990 was characterized by improved quality of life and growing inequality of income, and at the same time by efforts to achieve greater equality of wealth. At the end of this period, socialism become very popular in response to the liberal wave of the 1980s (Ronald Reagan and Margaret Thatcher stimulated ownership among the general public of such things as houses and shares).

At the same time, organizations became more professional, use of the computer and computerization became more widespread, and people had increasing access to improved information. This led to a second wave of economic growth, which started in the middle of the 1970s and lasted until the end of the 1980s. This growth was characterized by flexibility (Japan set the tone with fast, flexible production methods), huge amounts of information at low cost through the use of computers, the emergence of world markets and adaptation on the part of consumers: consumption in order to consume – consumptionism. A desire for a high income – and the lifestyle that went with it – was prominent. This in turn led to a further segmentation of the market and differentiation in consumer demand. During this period the demand for unskilled labour fell as tasks became ever more specialized. This resulted in a shortage of some types of skills and a surplus of others. Finally, there was a growing need for qualified staff which led to a more highly educated population. All of these aspects influenced society and the individualization of the people, as well as having an indirect effect on welfare.

Post-Fordism can be characterized by several attributes:

- new information technologies;

- emphasis on types of consumers in contrast to previous emphasis on social class;

- the rise of the service and white-collar worker;

- the feminization of the workforce;

- the globalization of financial markets.

Source: Wikipedia on Fordism.

The sales issue, as sketched above, led to the rise of advertising and marketing in order to sell the products and to accentuate the distinction between the various products (if such actually existed). Products became increasingly identical, distinctions were achieved in how the consumer experienced and perceived the product. Increased quality of life and far-reaching efficiency in production led to a wave of new products and rapidly growing demand.

The sales economy of the post-Fordist period (1960–1990) led to scaling up in every area, in production and demand as well as retailing (franchise chains, department stores and internationalization). The small shopkeeper was either pushed out of business altogether or resorted to targeting niche markets or specific locations. There was less and less room for the small shopkeeper; from the local baker baking on the premises to the fruit and veg shop, they are all slowly disappearing from the streetscape. After the post-Fordist period, the (pre-) Internet period began. This resulted in a convergence of private and business interests (and private and working time) between cultures and societies and, in terms of the economy, between internationally oriented organizations. Technology was no longer used just to make processes more efficient but also to enable changes on the basis of new possibilities. This was the start of the era of large infrastructures. These were based on media (radio, satellite television), on communications (such as the mobile network) and information (the Internet). The characteristics of this period (from 1990 to 2008) are:

- The increasing power of the media (television leading the way, followed by written media).

  All developments have an effect upon each other and this helped speed up the change process. Knowledge of these influences was acquired through television, newspapers and later also the Internet. However, mobility also increased dramatically and people were able to see for themselves what was happening elsewhere, during their holidays or business trips. Improved communications (by telephone and later mobile telephones and the Internet) meant increased international discourse, resulting in a greater knowledge of other cultures and customs.

- Migration, especially economic migration, became increasingly commonplace. Countries collaborated at international level and borders starting disappearing, both within Europe and between western countries. With the removal of the Iron Curtain, Eastern Europe became accessible and Eastern Europeans became the new workers in Western Europe. The influx of cheap, unskilled, labour from the former Eastern Bloc countries had consequences for the Western workforce. However, the multicultural society flourished thanks to developments in the EU which made living and working in different countries very easy, along with the integration of the second and third generations of former immigrant workers

- The increased level of education and training in Western Europe made it progressively easier for Europeans to communicate with each other – with English as the principal common language. Organizations collaborated with each other in an international context, and ideas and customs were exchanged. Managers of international companies also went to work in other countries and shared their views and culture with their foreign counterparts. Increasing leisure time and improved quality of life meant people holidayed abroad more, giving them an insight into each other's lives and into foreign customs and cultures.

- Improved telecommunications, such as the mobile phone, made individual communication possible – any time and anywhere. The Internet developed into a low-threshold information network in which everyone could and wanted to participate.

- In politics there was a 'swing' to the left, socialism became increasingly important throughout Europe and in many countries socialists were in government. This resulted in different balances of power and, in terms of society, power structures were also transformed. Equality in terms of lifestyle and public participation in decision making were the clearest examples of this.

The credit crisis which began in 2008 marked the end of an era of major growth and fast-rising consumptive spending and the beginning of a new (world) order. The crisis demonstrates that organizations had become uncontrollable due to excessive specialization, the power of technology, internationalization and a strong focus on profits. Organizations were part of a widespread network of

Table 3.2   Historical development of retail and technology

	Marketing/Retail	Technology	Customers/Buyers
Restructure *2008*	Individualism of the buyer Interactive marketing Demand-oriented economics Transparency of supply International demand Individual supply	Internet, telecommunications grid computing, server- oriented computerization Mobility basis: information, interaction, users' support	Interactive, critical, well informed Proactive, moment-driven Splitting of rational and hedonistic shopping Individual, non-binding
Internet *Pre-Internet*	Breakthrough of Internet shopping Hedonistic shopping becomes the norm High streets lose power to attract CRM for direct communications and person-bound information		
1990 *After-Fordism*	Rise of direct communication Uniformity in supply Decrease in impact of advertising Reorientation of role and function of marketing Concentration in retail, franchise formulas Rise of shopping centres and increasing power of consumer Rise of target groups with own characteristics and wishes	Automation of processes and functions Workplace support Production automation and robotization Basis: efficiency and effectiveness Central computerization, computerization of activities, process-related activities Computerization is the replacement of mechanization and labour Basis: replacement of unskilled work and routine work	Target group experience Rising individualism Diversification on basis of age and gender Increasing welfare and luxury Association with brands for individuality
1960 *Fordism* *1940*	Mass supply and mass consumption Rise of mass media and advertising Rise of large retail department stores Strong need for growth and integration Strong local supply and first self-service America as the guiding light in Europe	Mechanization Introduction of machines and process-oriented robots Assembly-line work Extensive mass production and standardization Basis: standardization, replacement of work and routine work	Exemplary function, leading, role pattern, the influence of advertising is strong Strong binding with shops and brands (trust) Rational shopping (because it is necessary)

companies, structures and people in power. Businesses also suffered under the power of a few who placed management bonuses above the general interests of an organization and above the interest of stakeholders such as employees or customers.

Since the 1990s there had been a strong focus on shareholder value, whereby the value of the organization, the profitability and the share prices were the primary concern. Decision makers were rewarded on the basis of these values (especially on share prices). Specialization had led to the creation of experts in very specific areas – their focused area of knowledge meant their managers and directors knew little about their day-to-day work. The crisis in the banking world has made this very clear. These experts developed products that no one understood anything about, only the profits (and therefore the bonus) counted. This meant the experts were not monitored and could therefore do what they wanted. The consequences of this became clear in 2008. No one understood anything any more – especially not the company directors – the final result was used as a measure of success; especially the measure that could be monitored, namely turnover and profits. When it turned out that various content constructions existed that were not beneficial to the business, and that financial products (with a composition unknown to many) were being offered, this led to a crisis of confidence. This crisis was worsened by the fact that frauds came to light (notably Madoff)[13] and that companies turned out not to be recession proof on account of a variety of financial structures (including Woolworths).

Since the 1990s, the role of the financial decision maker, the Chief Financial Officer (CFO) had grown ever greater.

The CFO was often the most powerful person when it came to making decisions concerning investments, organization structuring and marketing. Managers became responsible for budget and were results driven, typical characteristics of the Anglo-Saxon model, which is hardly surprising considering the interest American companies had in international trade and the exemplary function fulfilled by the USA. However, American culture is still different

---

13 Bernard Lawrence 'Bernie' Madoff is an American former stocbroker, investment adviser, non-executive chairman of the NASDAQ stock market, and the admitted operator of what has been described as the largest Ponzi scheme in history. In March 2009, Madoff pleaded guilty to 11 federal crimes and admitted to turning his wealth management business into a massive Ponzi scheme that defrauded thousands of investors of billions of dollars. Madoff said he began the Ponzi scheme in the early 1990s. However, federal investigators believe the fraud began as early as the 1980s, and the investment operation may never have been legitimate. The amount missing from client accounts, including fabricated gains, was almost $65 billion. *Source*: Wikipedia on Bernie Madoff.

to European culture and to British norms and values. In the retail trade, the refinancing of organizations in the 1990s was the most significant change.

More and more often, financing companies such as private investors and hedge funds owned the retail businesses and they wanted to see profits. Own equity was often replaced by outside capital, resulting in retail companies incurring high-interest debts. Own equity was also turned into cash through the sale of shop buildings – these same buildings were then leased back (sale- and leaseback models). This resulted in a rise in the fixed costs and reduced the flexibility of the retail organization. When the market shrank in 2008 and 2009 these organizations came under pressure. It's not hard to guess what the consequences of this were: extensive cost-saving measures, reductions in staffing and price increases to maintain the profit margin. These consequences will continue to be felt in the coming years as a result of reorganizations and bankruptcies.

QUELLE, KARSTAD AND THOMAS COOK ON THE VERGE OF BANKRUPTCY

Arcandor has applied for suspension of payment. As a result, well-known German retail businesses such as Karstad, Quelle and Thomas Cook are heading for bankruptcy. Some 70,000 members of staff risk losing their jobs; a huge blow to the German retail trade. A massive debt of 900 million euros turned out to be unfinanceable. There is nothing left to do except to sell off parts of the concern or simply apply for bankruptcy. This development is worrying for the entire German retail trade, which is going through difficult times. In that respect the situation is comparable to the Netherlands. Although there have not yet been any major bankruptcies, it seems that the coming months will be an anxious time for the retail trade in the Netherlands. If sales stagnate and the stocks can't be sold, then companies here will also end up with financing problems. If the stock remains unsold, no new winter collections can be bought and the situation would then become very worrying. It's typical that now, as I write at the beginning of the summer holidays, the first winter collections have already been spotted in the shops. Whichever way you look at it, this is a bad sign; for the retailers who are having to use summer sales space for winter clothing, and for consumers who haven't yet even started thinking about the winter yet (but once the clothing has been sold then payment can be made). It certainly seems that both sides would benefit from a better match between customer mood and the range on offer in the shops. But whatever the case, the coming months will be anxious, especially as reports on the recession are not getting any more optimistic.

Source: Various publications, June 2009.

The Current Position

The role of the Internet has also become increasingly important. Suddenly everything is available and transparent. People have become articulate and as such, in whatsoever role, have an opinion on developments and act accordingly: aversion against leaders, against bonuses and environmental violations, to give but a few examples. The Internet era has started and this marks the end of an industrial era.

The AF (after-Ford) period ended around 1990 and evolved smoothly into the pre-Internet era. Mechanization (Fordism) was firstly replaced by automation of processes (after-Fordism) and subsequently by the computerization of (tele)communications (large networks). The pre-Internet period is characterized by the implementation of networks, such as the introduction of (tele)communications with call centres and mobile phones.

Interactivity has become ever more important, accessibility and drive for momentum are the core concepts of this period, as is opportunism on the basis of the new technology and new possibilities. The introduction of the Internet has inspired young people to devise new concepts on the basis of technical possibilities. This has created expectations of an unbelievably rapid growth with corresponding profitability.

Thanks to the Internet, the world is suddenly the working domain and hundreds of millions of people are the target group. Creative spirits are devising totally different business propositions, new business models are not based on profitability but on growth and potential. The only companies to make these promises come true are based on normal business principles and based on needs; Amazon.com, Yahoo, along with MSN and Microsoft are among these 'good old companies'. Most of the new dotcom companies went out of business in the shake-out of 2002. That year showed the return of 'normal' business. It was no longer a case of playing around with the most creative concepts; it was business as usual again. Investments had to be profitable within a reasonable period and the Internet was a network that encompassed the world, but most business was still done locally. Reality kicked in and doing business through the Internet was once again based on traditional principles and on customer requirements.

New start-ups are not based on creative possibilities but on consumer needs. Most new entrepreneurs (the majority of whom are women) start their company from a personal need. It soon became evident that they were not the only ones with this need and their companies grew. Examples of this on a world scale include Google (the need for a good search machine) and Facebook (the need for a friend). In the same way, in fact, as with the introduction of new technologies; the first phase is one of experimentation, followed by an entrepreneurial phase, before the real growth phase starts.

The Internet is clearly now at the end of the entrepreneurial phase: many newcomers, specific markets and experimentation with the possibilities of technology based on recognized needs. It's often young entrepreneurs (under 35) who are entering the market now. This is where the basis for future development lies and in this phase customer orientation is high. From this phase (which is now coming to an end) large companies will grow and secure a dominant position (such as Google and Yahoo); other companies will occupy a dominant local position, and some companies will remain successful niche players. Most companies will remain small, successful or otherwise.

In all instances, the development of the Internet will lead to a restructuring of business life. The Internet has too great an impact on organizations and on the demand from the market, so companies simply must ensure that the technology (Internet) is embedded into the operational management. This period is also a new beginning for the retail trade. The market has reacted enthusiastically to the possibilities of the Internet as an information and sales medium, leading to a decline in the turnover of physical sales outlets. This hurts, and is made worse still by the recession of 2008! Now is the time to change and to redefine positions (restructuring). In the coming years, the retail trade will make choices that will determine the future of shopping. However, in contrast to other times, it's no longer the retail sector that defines what will happen but the customer, and the customers don't want boring shops or a multichannel strategy. Customers just want to be recognized as individuals, wherever they are!

The Convergence

The current period (post-2008) is a period of restructuring. The new infrastructures have matured and customers are implementing the possibilities they offer in their own manner. In recent years it has been evident that infrastructures are converging. Telephoning through the Internet is already possible (Skype for instance), it's possible to watch television via satellite or the

Internet (even if it's only to catch up on missed episodes) and use of the Internet via cable, mobile phone and satellite has become commonplace.

The use of the various infrastructures grew towards each other and converged. In fact this is standard for the development of new techniques. Initially there is separate development based on old structures in which the new techniques are used in a traditional manner. The following phase is when the user adapts the use to the possibilities of the technology and finally there is a convergence in which the technologies coalesce in user possibilities. The user then no longer notices the underlying technology (with an international telephone conversation you don't know whether it is by cable or by satellite).

> *The move online seems unavoidable, but a few retailers are still resisting it. So far, Primark, which says it has 'no plans for an online platform', seems unconcerned, as does H&M, which has websites in the Nordic countries but no plans to launch one for UK customers this year. 'The focus is on the stores – we are planning 225 new stores worldwide,' a spokesperson says.*

Source: *Daily Telegraph*, 3 February 2009.

In the coming years this convergence will be increasingly visible. Changes happen when there is a need for them, or when they are opportune or desired. It is precisely the recession of 2008–2009 that makes these changes possible. In order to survive, applying old methods and keeping old structures intact is not enough any more; there has to be a fundamental change.

For the retail sector, the development of e-commerce and remote buying will lead to a revolution. This development was initially regarded as a separate market, with a different target group and different products (the mail order target group). The impact of the Internet, however, made this channel increasingly important, and it has become a threat to the existing retail trade. This is evident in the shift in retail turnover, customers negotiating shop prices, and the shift in demand from physical shops to Internet retailers. To counter this, existing shops have also started offering their goods on the Internet. However, the Internet is a different world. Customers want different services, are open and direct, and also give their opinion instantly – having to wait for a response leads to irritation and orders must be dispatched quickly to avoid customer dissatisfaction. This demands quite a lot of adapting from an existing retailer wanting to offer their goods on the Internet. Dual channels raise a lot of very specific problems, such as opening times, e-mail response times, order picking and packing, return shipments and payments, to name but a few. It's also difficult to successfully pursue a dual channel strategy. We will examine the problems and developments associated with this in Chapter 5.

The answer to these problems is twofold: endemic or cross-channel? With an endemic approach, you make sure that you excel in what you are good at. This could be the channel, the product, the target group, the product range or perhaps the location (surroundings). Excelling in these areas will create a distinction in the eyes of the customer. A different channel should then support these excellent components. For instance, the Internet might only provide information about the shop or the opening times. Companies that clearly excel in the physical world include Zara for clothing and Mediamarkt for electronic goods. Zara is favourably priced and continually surprises customers with a new collection (monthly). Zara does not advertise so you have to go to the store to see what's in stock. Thanks to the attractive price you can also afford to buy more and you don't need to wear the clothes threadbare to get your money's worth.

Abercrombie&Fitch is a typical 'experience' shop. Emotion and experience lead to purchases. Impulse buys are an important component of this shopping experience.

In the case of cross-channel, the business model needs to be reconsidered and then, on the basis of this, it will be necessary to define where the focus should lie, how this can be achieved, which technologies could be implemented and how this will affect processes and structures. This entails a structural approach in which optimal use can be made of all the available technologies and infrastructures. Chapter 5 will discuss this convergence in the retail sector. It particularly examines customer behaviour and customer needs. Everything is related to these issues. This will be an important development for the retail sector en route to 2020 (the Internet era). Thus a tripartite supply market emerges:

ENDEMIC

- Parties that operate in the physical world only: At most, the Internet fulfils a supportive role in this physical proposition. The business model will be very similar to the current business model.

- Parties that operate on the Internet only and that make use of the possibilities and limitations of the Internet.

CROSS-CHANNEL

- The convergence, cross-channel, a combination of the Internet and a physical shop, in which the customer is the focal point. The Internet and other infrastructures are an integral part of the business model (thus also the physical location) based on customer needs and the systems, structures and processes related to that. The Internet is integrated within the physical shop and the physical shop is supplementary to the Internet proposition.

Tracy and Wiersema (1995)[14] assumed value disciplines that define the competitive power: operational excellence, customer intimacy and product leadership. The basis for the value disciplines is the underlying operational working model of an organization consisting of: processes, the organizational structure, management system and culture. By switching from an endemic organization to a cross-channel organization the value discipline has to be redefined and the underlying working model has to be tested and, if necessary, modified in order to be truly successful.

This is why restructuring is part and parcel of the Internet period (2008–2020). In order to survive the retailer has to decide what is really important: the competitive strategy and the underlying working model. This is the total entity with which a place in the commercial world has to be secured and a portion of the customer budget has to be achieved. The world has changed because of the changing market conditions, the different buying behaviour and the impact of the infrastructures on customers. In this new ecostructure choices once again have to be made. 'Why should customers buy from me?' is a question that needs to be posed again. It's only when this can be answered correctly and retailers are prepared to adapt the proposition, location, channels, assortment and customer approach accordingly that they can survive. It is, after all, the survival of the fittest.

---

14 Fred Wiersema & Michael Tracy, *Discipline of Market Leaders*, Addison-Wesley Publishing Company, Reading 1995.

Adaptation in Order to Survive

Fordism (1940–1960)

Focus: mechanization replaces labour, mass production.

Retail: small shops, first supermarket, increased size of shops, first specific shopping centres.

post-Fordism (1960–1990)

Focus: automation, efficiency processes and production.

Retail: rise of shopping centres, large growth of department stores (diversification), international collaborations, shopping becomes recreation.

Pre-Internet (1990–2008)

Focus: infrastructure, information, communication.

Retail: internationalization of chain stores, rise of e-commerce, uniformity in (physical) shops on high street, high level of prosperity, rise of small suppliers on the Internet (innovators), switch from supply-driven to demand-driven.

Internet (2008–2020)

Focus: convergence, adaptation of structure to suit infrastructure.

Retail: cross-channel retailing, focus on customer relations, integration of technology within buying behaviour, shake-out of suppliers on the Internet and growth (merging) of Internet suppliers, tripartite retailing (layering), physical retail, Internet retail and cross-channel (the break through of shopping 3.0).

Summary

- If the market changes, the retailer must ask themself whether change is also useful. It's not a must, but it must be a conscious choice.

- Customer buying behaviour has changed considerably, as have buying motives. Shops have to become attractive and congenial again, a meeting place where you can also buy things.

- Retailers must proactively respond to the needs and wishes of customers. Internet can be a choice, as can no Internet. For the customer it's not a question of choice, it's simply become part of a buying process.

• If in the coming years the new infrastructures converge, this will lead to even more opportunities and even more threats. Be aware of these and ask yourself how you can deal with them: advertise on the Internet with video clips, use the mobile phone for news and messages and narrowcasting in shops.

• Start by recording customer data and communicating directly, by e-mail, newsletter, website or ordinary letter. Communication enables you to build on your relationships, both private and business. Make sure that you can be found through entries on local sites and specific search sites.

DIGITAL NATIVES, THE YOUNG GENERATION BUYS DIFFERENTLY

Digital natives have been brought up in a different culture to the generations before them. Technology such as mobile phones, the Internet and online gaming have allowed children to communicate with each other and be entertained without leaving the house. Education began when people learnt how to read and write. The educational system was based around reading a book and learning to remember and write it back. This evolved into the classroom and hours spent every day learning through reading. It is not a natural born ability to be able to read, it is taught. In the exact same way, children now spend hours in the day playing on computers. It is the digitalized version of the book. This different lifestyle means that information is processed at a far greater speed and simultaneous bits of information can be absorbed. The major benefit of the Internet is that it allows several sources to be reached in seconds, a far more affective method than a library. With this in mind, it is necessary for education to be changed in order to more directly stimulate the digital natives. New techniques must be found to reach children's different cognitive skills. Therefore in order to educate them, a far more interactive and entertaining method must be found than reading books.

Source: Thesis, Digital natives and digital immigrants. RSM students: Sarah Gobeil Boulanger and Benjamin Dineen.

'BEST BUY' IN ENGLAND

A retail park in Essex is the unlikely scene for a shopping revolution, but that's exactly what Best Buy is hoping to achieve with the opening of its first UK store near Thurrock. The consumer electronics chain has already enjoyed huge success in the US, where it has earned a reputation for excellent customer service and a competitive pricing strategy, and it's hoping to muscle in on the turf currently occupied by the likes of Currys and Dixons.

Best Buy's Blueshirts – its cadre of shop assistants – undergo an intensive nine-week training course to ensure they are well-versed in the nuances of customer care. They're the front-line warriors who must recommend the right products and deliver the 'retail experience' that Best Buy is striving for.

However, in the Internet age, where consumers are becoming increasingly confident about buying things online, do high-street retailers have a future?

Kevin Styles, Marketing Director at Best Buy, certainly thinks so. 'We're all about show, not tell,' he says. 'That's why we've divided the store in to different areas, such as gaming, or home theatre, with plenty of space for customers to try out products for themselves so they can make a decision.'

'We have a service called 'Walk out Working' – buy a device from us, and we'll ensure you leave the shop with your phone or laptop loaded with the apps and software you need to just start using it.'

According to the Office of National Statistics, less than 5 per cent of retail sales, for any products, take place online. However, consumer electronics is one of the most popular categories for online shopping, with people snapping up everything from digital cameras to fridge-freezers on the web. The latest figures from market research firm GfK show that almost a quarter of all sales of digital imaging products, such as cameras, photo printers and accessories, were made online.

'Shopping online brings some huge benefits,' says David Smith, Director of Operations at IMRG, which represents the e-retail industry. 'The biggest advantage is the speed and convenience with which you can shop around for the best price. You can also do lots of your own product research online.'

In these credit-crunched times, of course, cost is a key consideration, and online-only retailers who don't have to pay for physical stores are perhaps better-placed to offer bigger discounts, but price is not the only issue, says Simon Harper, a partner in the retail division at analysts Booz & Co.

'Someone buying a CD player or DAB radio online will behave quite differently to someone spending thousands of pounds on a new TV,' he says. 'There are lots of different categories of consumer, some of whom feel comfortable buying things online, but many of whom don't.'

'For people who don't shop online, in-store customer service is crucial – it's about educating and offering advice, and ensuring they get the right product. Those who do shop online might prefer to do their research in-store first, then make the purchase over the Internet; others are happy to research products independently on the net and buy them online.'

'Companies such as Best Buy and John Lewis are aiming for the best of both worlds – competitive online prices with a service-orientated offering in-store.'

For Robbie Feather, Buying Director for the home and electricals division at John Lewis, differentiating on service and price is crucial, whether shoppers are buying online or on the high street. 'We offer free delivery, a flexible returns policy and extended guarantees on televisions, DVD players, camcorders, hi-fis and PCs,' he says.

In some cases, though, could such excellent customer service be a double-edged sword? Shoppers might be tempted to use stores such as John Lewis or Best Buy as a research facility, testing out the latest products to decide which one to buy before shopping online for the cheapest deal.

Indeed, Dixons recently run an advertising campaign poking fun at the likes of John Lewis and Selfridges, suggesting that shoppers go in to those stores to take advantage of their expertise, but then buy the product online from Dixons for less.

Feather is reluctant to talk about rivals' marketing initiatives, but thinks the campaign raised an interesting point. 'We know from our customers that they value service above anything else, so we do find it a bit odd that another business would try to make a virtue of the fact that they don't have anything like a comparable service.'

It seems that whether you prefer to buy online or in-store, shops will be bending over backwards to ensure you have the right information to make a purchase – and that they offer enough 'added value' to ensure you make that purchase with them.

Source: Daily Telegraph, 1 May 2010.

4

Customers Want Recognition: Making the Shopping Experience Personal

Customers simply want to be recognized as individuals, wherever they are! This is a challenge for the retail sector; not only do you have to recognize customers when they enter your shop but also if you bump into them elsewhere. This used to mean that you had to recognize your customers in a private setting; such as on the football field or in church. Nowadays, the Internet plays a significant role. Recognition on the Internet must include recognition in the shop and vice versa. The customer feels the bond, the customer has loyalty because of the range of goods and services, the shopkeeper or the staff or the perception. The customer wants to have this commitment confirmed by recognition, appreciation and a sense of friendship.

Customers can sometimes speak quite emotionally about their preferred brand or shop, and the retailer should be proud. However, the context has become much larger. When operating at a local level a particular image and reputation can be cultivated, but if the market area becomes diffuse this is much more difficult. Retailers have to use other means to sustain customer loyalty. This loyalty could be sought in hedonistic (fun) aspects of making shopping attractive, in specialist aspects to ensure the range is distinctive, or in loyalty aspects that stimulate and motivate the bond.

Shopping at Local Shops?

Retailing on the basis of experience is no longer sufficient. Retailers have to deal with different kinds of customers, with different buying motives and different buying behaviour. It's increasingly difficult for retailers to bind customers to their shop by traditional means (physical and personal) and to really know the customer. Mobility makes it possible to travel further than before, city shopping a hundred kilometres away in, say, London, Manchester or Newcastle is simple. Shopping is often combined with a day out or a family visit. How, then, are retailers supposed to know their customers?

In the past customers had very little choice. Limited mobility and a close-knit community meant that people always shopped in their own village. This 'prisoners' situation was generally accepted. Travel into town was reserved for special purchases and going to the neighbouring village was out of the question – that would lead to gossip. Shopping locally still happens in villages and small towns but this is usually due to personal circumstances – people with young families and immobile elderly people may find that this is more convenient for them. However, nowadays, senior citizens are in better health and are more mobile than in previous generations, thanks to subsidized taxis, local buses and, of course, their own cars. On top of which, they have plenty of time so shopping becomes quite an outing and includes a break for refreshments.

The division between work and home also means that purchases are not made locally. Groceries are often bought during the lunch break or on the way home. Visting the shopping centre near the office with colleagues can be fun. Often, only the most urgent grocery shopping is done locally. Additionally, general prosperity can mean that more is purchased than is strictly necessary. Shopping is seen more and more as a hobby, with celebrities, in particular, setting the tone. Exclusive shops, like those in Regent Street or Bond Street in London, appeal to large sections of the population. On the one hand, people allow themselves the luxury because they have to work hard for it, on the other it's also a way of distinguishing yourself from the masses. Brands are increasingly regarded as proof of social status and social association, as discussed in Chapter 1.

The developments that affect traditional retailing were first prompted by a different buying behaviour, changed buying motivation and a different range of mobility. This customer behaviour shift started the change, but it was intensified by the Internet.

Changes in the (Retail) Channel

In the last decade particularly (since 2002), non-store retailing has become a fully-fledged retail channel with its own suppliers, products and customs.

Retailers were surprised by these developments and were extremely slow in their response. Some retail branches were affected by the Internet and its effect sooner than others (Figure 4.1).

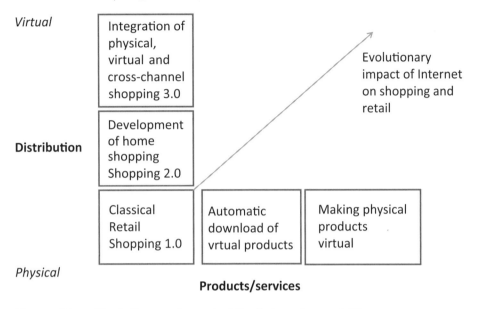

Figure 4.1   Evolutionary impact of the Internet on retailing

The impact of the Internet on the retail trade first became noticeable as a result of the modification of existing processes and functions, this later led to a modification in products. In the end there will be harmony between the virtual and the physical, albeit within a new structure.

The impact of the Internet was first seen with regard to rational products that could be bought without any problems. Books and music (CDs) are the best examples of this. There is little or no risk involved and customers know precisely what they want. The developments in these two branches are illustrative of possible developments in other markets and the impact thereof on the existing retail trade. Music and books were the frontrunners in the changes that occurred through the impact of Internet, but each one had its own cause and consequence. With books it was mainly the simplicity of buying books that boosted book sales on the Internet (the development on the vertical axis of the model). With music it was actually digitization that led to changes (the development on the horizontal axis of the model). If you already know which book you want you can buy it faster online.

Amazon.co.uk became the market leader, following the example of Amazon.com in the USA. The founder of Amazon started the online bookshop because he was unable to buy certain books in the village where he lived. The idea of selling books through the Internet stemmed from this frustration. The launch of Amazon meant anyone could buy books, no matter where they were. The success was quickly apparent and for years Amazon was the fastest-growing Internet shop. It is still a world player today, setting an example for many other suppliers.

The resulting changes in the book trade were first apparent in the distribution channel. The new suppliers could deliver many books very quickly, often even the next day. Amazon.com made it possible to view the entire range of published (English language) books at once. This meant that customers could look for books themselves and were no longer dependent on what the local bookshop had in stock. It might appear a minor change, but it was a change that was to set the tone for the Internet. Existing retailers saw part of their turnover disappear; in particular, textbooks and bestsellers were bought this way, thus eroding the profit margins of the bookshops. A number of significant restrictions affected book retailers in particular:

- The bookshop only had a small proportion of all the available books in stock. Of all the available titles a bookshop might have, say, 3,000 books in stock and only a limited number of copies of each title.

- Many books have a low turnover speed but as there are also bestsellers with a high turnover speed, an average profitability can still be achieved. If these bestsellers and textbooks (which were often sold to order) were removed then that would leave only books with a low turnover speed and books with a high impulse factor.

The impact online sales had on existing bookshops was therefore considerable. It was a typical example of adaptation to survive. The new suppliers on the Internet opted for rational purchases and offered an unlimited range. High levels of service were given to customers by means of the extra information that was provided about the book and its author, often with the aid of the publisher, but also of the author as well. Reviews of the book also provided an impression of what other people thought of it (although everyone knew that this was manipulated).

Through this information the customer got to know more about the book and the author than they would have through their local book retailer. Additionally, the delivery process had been optimized – order today, delivered tomorrow! These advantages are typical of Internet shops. They could be described as endemic suppliers (suppliers who only occur in one world: the Internet), and are also called 'pure players' who draw their strength from the opportunities provided by the Internet.[1] Indeed, these circumstances only apply to the Internet. Switching to the physical world is difficult because other rules apply there.

The response of the physical shops was threefold, depending on the company strategy and the customers:

- optimization of the existing sales point;

- realigning the range on offer to the customers (target group) and the buying moment;

- online support.

THE WRITING WAS ON THE WALL FOR BORDERS' BUSINESS MODEL

By Nicholas Paisner, 27 November 2009

Borders UK did not collapse because it was massively overleveraged or even because of the recession.

The private-equity backed bookseller suffered from an old-fashioned problem: its business model no longer worked.

Administrators have stepped in after efforts to find a buyer for the business failed. Hilco, a UK buy-out and advisory firm specializing in distressed retail, may have underestimated the extent of Borders' troubles when it backed a management buy-out six months ago. That was two years after the US Borders Group sold the company to UK private-equity firm Risk Capital.

---

1   The word endemic is derived from biology and indicates that plants or animals are found in one place only. Darwin encountered endemic species on each of the Galapagos Islands. Endemic suppliers are similarly bound to the possibilities of an ecosystem. This can be the Internet where they make use of all the advantages of the Internet and through this specialism have extra competitive strength in the same way as the animals were able to use the ecological conditions of the island to their advantage (by adaptation and evolution). Suppliers whose strength lies in the physical world have problems with the Internet because different rules apply there.

The business suffered from many of the same difficulties as other retailers. Consumers have been tightening their belts, while high-street rents remain high, especially in prime locations such as London's Oxford Street. But the industry has also been wrestling with its own set of problems.

Sales have migrated to online retailers and supermarkets. Trade journal *The Bookseller* estimates Amazon now handles almost 20 per cent of sales in the UK's £1.9bn book market, only slightly behind the share of retail leader Waterstones. For some popular titles, supermarkets pile 'em high and sell 'em cheap – taking more than 50 per cent of the market.

The high-street trade is squeezed. Waterstone's has managed to hold on, with only a 3 per cent decline in sales in continuing stores in the year that ended in April. Book-lovers complain it has made it by going downmarket.

When the UK first allowed publishers to sell books to favoured retailers at a discount, back in 1997, the US Borders Group saw an opportunity. It misread the effect of the change.

Administrators hope to keep Borders trading, but it will face yet another competitor – electronic readers such as Amazon's Kindle. Once again, in the UK, it looks like Waterstone's is a step ahead of its high-street rivals. It has agreed to distribute Sony's rival e-reader and offer access to 19,000 titles. But that still looks like a relatively unexciting offering.

From a strictly commercial perspective, the woes of Borders are just a sign of the times. The likes of Dan Brown won't be fazed by the news. But for authors hoping to sell anything less popular, life has just got a little harder.

Source: *Daily Telegraph*, 27 November 2009.

Optimization of the Sales Point

The locally oriented bookshop has disappeared from the streetscape. Large chains of bookshops such as WH Smith and Barnes & Noble have been converted into multimedia experience worlds where customers can spend hours browsing through books. The staff are extremely competent and you can leaf through the books and purchase and take them with you. This is an upgrading of the existing channel. However, the competition has also been felt by these large chains. Indeed, because these companies distinguished themselves with their attractive shops in A1 locations (busy shopping streets), transferring their stores to the Internet was not immediately a good option for them. They sought physical resilience, to enhance their competitive strength in the physical world. Large shops, in A1 locations with extremely competent staff have always been an important weapon in the competitive battle. By going online with a me-too product, retailers may, in fact, lose competitive strength. Many have made the decision to upgrade their existing stores providing new shop layouts and furnishings, better ambience and relaxing corners with a Starbucks inside.

However, the decision has also been made to reduce costs by utilizing advanced technology. This is RFID technology which enables improved order processing and improved stock management. By affixing the (practically invisible) RFID tag to the books, it's possible to track where the books are on the shelves. Stocktaking can now be done in a fraction of the time than was previously needed, which means weekly updates are possible. This RFID technology has optimized the shop and the traditional customer contact.

Realigning the Range on Offer to the Buying Moment

The existing retail trade is adapting to the new customer buying behaviour (and the impact of the Internet) by focusing on the buying moment. This buying moment is crucial, especially with emotion-based purchases, because the customer is in an emotional lock-in situation. I want it and I want it NOW. This moment is encouraged by a good store layout, the right product range, special offers and an optimal ambience. Articles should be on show, ready to be picked up and tried on if needed.

Online Support

The existing traditional retailers are, of course, considering the possibilities of the Internet. The existing physical bookshops on the Internet often play a supportive role to the proposition in the shop. Orders can be placed, books reserved and information obtained. Customers buying through these sites will often collect the book in the shop. The Internet has therefore become a new way of ordering books, replacing in-store ordering. The shop remains the point of contact for these customers. This is a good combination of the physical strength of the shop with support through the Internet (cross-channel). This is a better and more favourable proposition than trying to compete against the Internet suppliers.

Some market leaders on the Internet are very dominant. Fighting these businesses is difficult because they always attract the most customers and have the most customer information. They also often have a high recognition factor and a top-of-mind position amongst Internet users. The opportunity for new entrants lies in providing distinctive goods; becoming a niche player, focusing entirely on a particular segment and becoming the market leader in that segment. By only offering very specialized items there is a greater focus on the intended target group, and this creates a connection with the customers. It's funny really, because the Internet has no stock limitation, every supplier can, in effect, offer everything. Market leader Amazon can therefore offer 3 million book titles and also expand its range of goods constantly by adding other product groups. The result is that Amazon is becoming more and more of a media department store where the customer has to find his way around. Niche players specialize in a particular segment, which is then expressed in the limited range, in the goods offered on the home page and the look and feel of the site; a commercial rationale. Hence they capitalize on the feelings of the target group on the basis of the contact that occurs when you visit the site.

JOHN LEWIS REVAMPS FASHION WEBSITE AND TESTS LUXURY AREA IN STORES

LONDON – John Lewis has overhauled its online fashion site as part of a move to support a new 'luxury' concept in womenswear.

The retailer aims to add £70m in fashion sales by 2011 and is adding 100 new brands online which cover womenswear, menswear, accessories, childrenswear and beauty.

The revamped site, which launches today, will also provide seasonal trend guidance to consumers, provided by Marie O'Riordan, Editor in Chief of John Lewis' *Edition* magazine. 'Brand Boutiques' will present online customers with virtual shop windows in which to browse. It will also have magazine-style pages that will feature regularly changing style guides, encouraging customers to put outfits together as they browse.

John Lewis is also implementing a 'luxury shop' area in its womenswear floors starting with John Lewis Cardiff, opening on 24 September. This includes a designer area, contemporary fixtures for jewellery and accessories, a denim wall and a feature ceiling. The concept has no defined walkways, allowing shoppers a sense of discovery.

The concept has been incorporated into the refurbishment of John Lewis Bluewater and if successful it will be rolled out to the majority of branches during the next two years.

The changes come as the retailer spends a record amount on advertising this autumn, as it looks to boost its fashion credentials. Earlier this month it also launched a new customer lifestyle magazine, called *John Lewis Edition*.

Source: www.marketingmagazine.co.uk, 14 September 2009.

The Impact of the Internet

The changes in the book trade as a result of the Internet are very clear: fewer physical bookshops, a restyling of large existing bookshops and an adaptation to the buying behaviour and buying motives by offering more 'emotion' and 'moment' products. The impact of the Internet is principally an impact on distribution; customers can buy from home and receive the book the next day. But this is actually the optimization of existing structures; there hasn't been any real change – that is still to come! In the music retail sector this change *is* already visible. The impact of the Internet was initially limited to the distribution function; CDs were sold on the Internet instead of in the shop. But music was split into three components and change soon followed:

- the listening/playing component;

- the music medium;

- the music (content).

Changes occurred in all three of these components as a result of technological developments and the Internet. With a few years the listening/playing component has changed from a physical component for a physical music carrier to a component for a virtual music medium. The record player with a gramophone record became a CD player and CD. This first step was not a structural change; merely a technological modification. The CD stored the music digitally instead of analogously. This digital music store could also be sent digitally and stored on other mediums.

Initially, in the 1990s, CDs were burned on a large scale. Digital music was copied from one CD to the other. This intermediate step became superfluous with the rise of the mp3 player and later disappeared altogether following the introduction of the iPod, which was loaded digitally through the Internet and could be changed at will. The playing component changed therefore from a player to a combined player and music carrier (an integrated product). The music was no longer tied to a component but was unravelled into separate pieces (numbers), making it virtual, and could be sold and sent through the Internet. The music sector changed dramatically as a result. CDs were no longer bought (by the mass public); they were downloaded. When clever suppliers started offering these downloads for free, the business model was permanently undermined. Digitization of the product and an intangible, free supply meant the impact of the Internet on this market was harsh.

The book trade has not yet undergone this battle, but does have elements in it that indicate that the same could happen. A book also has two components:

- the medium, the book;

- the content, the text.

The medium, the book, is only slowly being replaced by other formats, such as the spoken book (audio book) and the e-book. But the book, and in particular the reading moment, is determinant. An audio book is handy in the car, which is why audio versions of management books are also being published. These are aimed at the businessman who spends a lot of time in his car, and are an ideal way of 'reading' professional literature. But the market for the audiobook will always be limited because books have a high emotion and moment factor:

- Business books are about the content and often about being able to find important information repeatedly. The split into audio (content) and a reference book is therefore logical.

- With literature a combination of content, re-reading and owning is important. A well-filled bookcase in the living room looks good but also serves a purpose. Knowledge is always readily available, searching for information can be done quickly (with traditional media) and re-reading a book is easy.

Moment books are books that are subject to fashion. These are often thrillers, love stories or popular stories. The time element is particularly important – losing yourself in a book, the holiday feeling. These are books you read and you don't really keep. In effect they are consumption books; the question is whether this should continue to exist as a book. Now it is often an impulse buy, at the station or the airport, so a book is the appropriate medium, but if it becomes a conscious choice then the Internet will again play an important role.

Physical books will find themselves competing with the e-book readers. These are a sort of compact computer with a high screen resolution so that you can also read in daylight and sunlight. The e-book reader enables you to store lots of books and read them whenever you want. You can also download new books from the Internet. The reading pleasure of an e-book reader is different to a book but certainly equivalent. This format works for books that only have to be read, that is, books where you don't need to mark up the text. E-readers are compact and fast to load, and e-books are often low cost, so that you can take hundreds of books with you on your travels. This creates a bridge between the physical books and the texts that you have to read on a computer screen. The new generation of e-book readers are also connected to the Internet so that a new book can be downloaded anywhere. This is not the only function of the e-book reader:

GET READY FOR THE NEWSSTAND IN YOUR HAND

The next generation of e-book readers will deliver colourful, interactive papers and magazines wirelessly.

British buyers may be only just getting their hands on a new range of e-book readers, but already the next generation of hardware has been revealed. At the giant Consumer Electronics Show (CES) in Las Vegas earlier this month, where the gadget industry previewed the next 12 months of innovation, e-book readers were the hottest product category. Dozens of new devices were unveiled, featuring everything from colour displays and flexible, shatter-proof screens to text-to-speech software and new ways to connect and share books over the Internet. And many fulfil the promise of being able to display daily, downloadable newspapers and magazines in the way the publications' designers intended.

E-BOOK REVOLUTION

The electronic versions of most books might still be as staid and monochrome as printed text itself, but they too are to get a makeover. Shown at CES were several types of software that, running on future e-readers, will bring web-like interactivity to novels and full-colour graphics to illustrated books.

Blio, for example, is designed for a future where black-and-white screens have been superseded by colour displays. It allows the publishers of highly illustrated volumes, such as children's books, to faithfully reproduce layouts. It will be free to download from February in the US.

Copia, meanwhile, combines e-book reader software and social networking, allowing users to join together in a massive online book club. From an e-reader you will be able to see what titles your friends have rated and add comments on any books you've read. It launches in the spring.

Source: *Sunday Times*, 17 January 2010.

News is created every minute, so why wait for the newspaper to read the full story with background information? Could it be a solution to continuously offer the newspaper as an e-book and keep updating it? This would enable the reader to specify their interests and receive information that is particularly of interest to them. Journalists could then offer the news in sections, supported by background information just like it is in the newspaper. The advantage is that the news would be offered on the basis of user preferences (profile) as it happens and could be read on an e-book reader.

The impact of the e-book is comparable to that of an mp3 player and may lead to major changes in journalism, for newspapers and also in the book sector. The impact is already evident in countries such as the USA and the UK where there are no fixed retail prices for books. The average book costs 20 euros whilst an e-book costs an average of 3 euros. The savings in terms of production and distribution costs are passed on directly to the reader. Newspapers are already feeling the impact of the Internet as an information medium, this has resulted in fewer subscribers, fewer advertisers and mass competition from free newspapers. The changes are already underway.

For other markets and products the developments are still limited and depend on how purchases are made and the possibility of digitalizing a product or service. As soon as this becomes partially or fully possible the impact of the Internet will be considerable, with direct consequences for the retail trade.

THE FUTURE

The future of e-books is one of the most contentious subjects in technology at the moment: later this month, Apple is set to announce its tablet computer, which is likely to do away with a keyboard and simply use a large, hand-held touch-screen. Some tech commentators believe that this bodes ill for e-Readers, however, others point out that the machines are part of the evolution of reading and will themselves continue to evolve. As David Kohn of Waterstone's points out: 'e-Books and e-Readers mark the biggest revolution in the way we read since the introduction of Penguin paperbacks in the 1930s.' Sales of e-Readers are on the rise and most computers have yet to be able to offer long battery life and easy-reading. In fact, if anything is holding e-Readers back it is not the threat from computers but instead from publishers: only as complicated problems surrounding software, piracy and price are resolved will common standards emerge and e-Readers become a mainstream gadget in their own right.

Source: Daily Telegraph, 22 January 2010.

Digitization

Digitization involves several different components: a product can be offered digitally, as is the case with music, games and now also with books and a digital product can be downloaded so that the need for physical distribution disappears completely. This is clearly evident with music; records used to be sold in shops, just like CDs. The Internet has changed distribution (buying): the physical product used to be bought on Internet and delivered to the home, now the product (music) has been disconnected from the medium, it's been made downloadable and physical distribution has become redundant (with all the related consequences for traditional retailers). The product has been digitized and can be bought online and downloaded.

The next development, now that the medium has been disconnected from the content, is the modification of the medium to listen to the content. Initially this was a generic computer, such as a laptop and nowadays the netbook, then came the specific medium, such as the mp3 player, which can be connected to the computer and hence directly to the Internet. The next phase will be a specific online medium. This will not only enable a direct connection to the Internet, but also a direct connection to the environment. This also makes it possible to respond to a person's mood or activity. After all, when you are running you listen to a different sort of music than when you are in the train or car. Mood, activity and location-driven preferences can therefore be defined.

The transformation then seems to be complete: the product is digitized, the purchase is made online and sometimes even continuously (use basis), and you define the moment of consumption yourself. Consumption then becomes personal, and defined by mood and location. The physical retail trade has been sidelined for this product, the physical retailers only have a role in respect of the traditional (and physical) product (selling CDs or selling mp3 players).

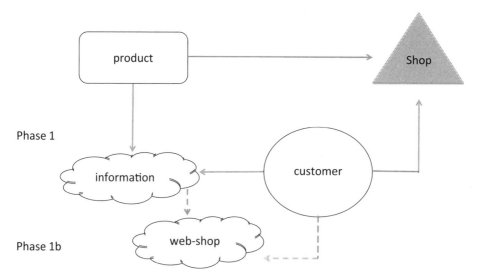

Figure 4.2   Phase 1, digitization of the buying processing and information

The music example is of course specific to the music sector, but it is nevertheless a clear example of the phases of development in digitization, as is also shown in Figure 4.2. Phase 1 is a physical product that is bought for a generic medium (computer). Specific information can be sought on the Internet. In phase 2 (see Figure 4.3) the product is digitized and is bought on the Internet for a specific medium (such as an mp3 player or e-book reader).

In phase 3 (see Figure 4.4) the medium is adapted to the use and the specific possibilities; the product can then also be further adapted (such as iTunes did by selling music as individual tracks instead of the whole album). Many products will go through a similar sort of development, with books, games and news leading the way. However, changes will also occur for other products as a result of digitization.

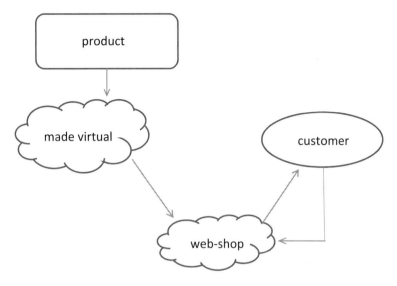

Figure 4.3   Phase 2, digitization of products, made downloadable

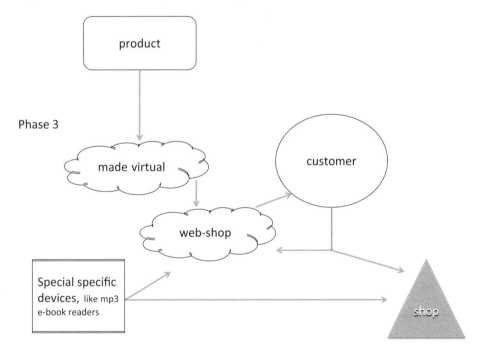

Figure 4.4   Phase 3, specific digital devices become available

In the next phase specific devices are developed for the now virtual products. Customer can buy on the Internet or in the shop. The device is physical again.

The First Phase of Change Distribution

The first phase of the impact of Internet has seen the development of e-commerce (this has happened during the pre-Internet phase from 1990–2008). During this phase the traditional retail trade found itself competing against the new distribution channel. Shopkeepers had to compete against unknown suppliers, customers buy wherever suits them best and at times that fit into their lifestyle (including evenings, weekends and even through the night). The change that occurred in the first phase mainly relates to the form of distribution.

The advantages for the customer are clear: plenty of suppliers, a surveyable range of goods and services, and transparency of both the range on offer and the price. Additionally, a lot of information is available to aid the purchase process. This can be product information, supplier and user information. The advancement of the informative function is also a development of uncontrolled, that is, unmonitored (information) supply, often frustrating the supplier. Users create their own weblog, customers post information in a guest book and sometimes on their own website. This information is naturally subjective, but because of the volume of information available on the Internet, customers can draw their own conclusions. They will also look for confirmation of their own opinion (or suspicion).

This first phase (the pre-Internet phase) represents a change in buying behaviour. The new form of distribution offers new possibilities for the customers: buy whenever you want, with no restrictions on what's on offer and the convenience of home delivery. In addition, there is a lot of information that the Internet user can access. Specialists are often challenged by users who have looked up information about products, services or medical problems, for example. The first phase of the impact led to articulate, well-informed and critical customers who determine for themselves what they purchase and where.

This phase actually only really began after the so-called Internet bubble burst in 2002. Up to that point the Internet was still very technology-driven and was not really accessible for the majority of the general public. As a result, the behaviour of only a small group – known as 'early adopters' – was influenced. In the last decade, however, the Internet has become widely accepted as a fully-fledged distribution and information channel. The impact on the retail trade is still only in the initial phase.

At present, retailers mainly feel the effect of the Internet as a distribution channel. This is apparent from the growth of both home shopping and buying through the Internet. The difference between the two being that traditional home shopping involves choosing and ordering the products by post and/or from mail order catalogues. Non-store retail sales rose in 2008 and 2009 by about 20 per cent. The forecast is that, in about 5 years time, approximately 30 per cent of non-food retail will be sold through the Internet. However, almost everybody will check the Internet first before buying anything. The impact of the Internet on retail is therefore bigger than ever. This will lead to more sales generally, more sales per customer, more repeat visits and, of course, more trust.

However, there is hope for existing retailers. Customers prefer to buy from the existing stores they are familiar with from the high street and at the web-shop of market leaders. Secondly, customers often prefer not to have the orders delivered to their home address – they may not be at home to take delivery because they are at work or out and about doing other things. Neighbours are not always willing to accept parcels for others and delivery drivers are frustrated by non-delivery. Pick-up places will be the solution. A pick-up place could be the local shop. Service points at petrol stations or supermarkets could be an option. Although the Internet is all about non-store retailing, retailers can play an important role as pick-up places, benefitting from traffic in their shop and the sale of add-ons!

The Japanese are known for their long working days and their preference for travelling on public transport. There is nearly always a 7-Eleven supermarket between the station and their home – these stores are typically open around the clock because most people return home very late and leave again very early in the morning. Eighty per cent of Internet purchases are picked up at the local 24/7 supermarket on the way home.

The Second Phase, Digitization

The second phase of change – the Internet phase which started in 2008 – is a phase of digitization, leading to a structural change in the customer buying process, and also in the goods and services offered by manufacturers and retailers. This phase occurs at different levels: the product can be offered digitally, the buying process can be digitalized and the medium can support specialist products and services.

Over the coming years this phase will lead to changes for many products and services both in the retail trade and the buying process. Digital products are virtual products like music, books, information and games, but also services such as navigation services. No physical context is required for this. The device will be adapted to the use and the user. However, the degree to which physical products also have a virtual element, such as information for example, will also be examined. A number of examples demonstrate these developments: watching a football game and being able to see the goals online or access background information; being able to see products in the shop and consult product information online; shopping in town and automatically being referred to the best offer; seeing a poster and, by scanning in a code at home, being able to view all the information through the Internet. These are all types of location-based services and product-based services. In these applications, the location or product is linked to the virtual information that is made available.

A good example, I think, is the support given with a Garmin watch when running. Through the link from the product to a satellite, and wirelessly to your chest band, you can read your heart rate, your running speed and the distance you've covered on your watch. If you have stored some general information it will also automatically calculate the calories burned. So when you get home after all your exertions, the data can be loaded directly to your own page at www.mygarmin.com and transferred so that you can compare it with earlier sessions or with the desired exertion (virtual partner). A link is also made with Google Earth so that you can go over your running route at leisure and see where the lactic acid build-up started.

Other examples of where this split between virtual and physical has been made often include service products linked to a physical product, such as Nespresso. The machine is sold in the shop and the customers can take advice and gather information. But you buy the actual coffee, the pads, on the Internet and they are delivered to your home. Through an online 'alert service' you are warned when your coffee is likely to run out.

Software and hardware suppliers also make use of this combination. The equipment is (often) bought in the shop, but there is an online registration of personal details. This enables the buyers to be kept up to date on new releases, service information or update options. Of course, this also means that the supplier will then have the customers' details and can send them newsletters. The customer is recognized online by the manufacturer, whereas they only used to be recognized by the shopkeeper.

This new possibility has created an area of tension between the shop and the supplier. After all, who has customer contact, the shop or the manufacturer? The physical product is delivered by the shopkeeper but the online services are delivered by the manufacturer. This generates a different sort of relationship between the shopkeeper and the manufacturer – in the most favourable cases to a mutual relationship based on communication with the customer. This is more difficult to demonstrate in the food sector, where customers buy from the grocery store but feel an (emotional) bond with the brand. However, in the non-food sector there are more possibilities for registering customer data. In fact, it is these developments outlined above where, in addition to a physical element there is also a virtual element, that lead to the bond being split. There is a bond on the basis of the physical product and a bond on the basis of other elements such as image, brand, services or fast delivery. But there is also a bond with the product and a separate bond with the shop.

Naturally, this has always been the case, but through the Internet it has entered a new dimension (virtual buying and virtual products). At the same time a new partnership arises between the shop and the supplier. The shop provides support to the physical product while services are supplied through the Internet. The old distribution channel is under pressure and this partnership remains in force only because the shopkeeper trusts the manufacturer not to start selling directly. Some suppliers are very strict (perhaps rigid) in executing this.

Bose, for instance, only sells through shops. Shops are not allowed to sell the products through the Internet, on pain of losing the dealership. This not only protects the existing channel but also Bose's philosophy: hearing is buying. Bose claims perfect sound quality that you have to experience for yourself, therefore you have to go to the shop. Bose is dependent on the expertise and loyalty of the shop and that is something they both protect and safeguard. If anything at all is available through the Internet, then these are very special products (like a stand alone alarm/audio combination) that cannot be bought through the shop. Bose is very clear in its distribution policy but it is based on a well-considered philosophy.

The impact of the Internet on the retail trade is only just emerging. The Internet is still only used for sales and communication. The first signs of a restructuring of the retail trade, through the Internet and through shopping 3.0 are already visible (see Figure 4.5). The period of restructuring and adaptation

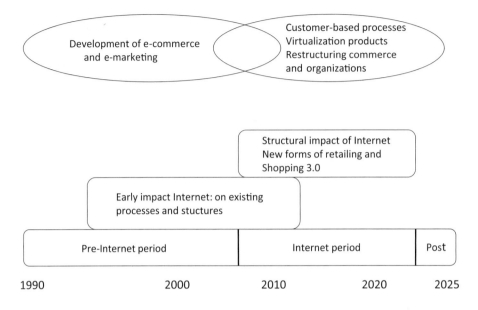

Figure 4.5   The pre- and post-Internet retail landscape

has commenced. It is now up to the retailer to see the possibilities and to respond to the new shopping behaviour of customers

More and more often physical elements will be separated from virtual elements or information elements. This enables changes in the distribution and in the registration of customer information. Direct communication on the basis of customer knowledge strengthens the relationship and supports the buying process. To provide the user with ever better service the medium will need to be adapted to specific wishes. A navigation system is an example of this; while you can navigate well enough using your laptop, a specific device (the TomTom) is better still, but in the future the medium of choice will be your smartphone. An mp3 offers more listening convenience than your computer, an e-book reader views better than your laptop and a notebook is not as handy as a netbook if you're often on the move and active on the Internet. New developments are coming up on the basis of the wishes of users, characteristics of customers and to support mobility. A few examples of developments to come:

1.   Biometric fingerprint payment.

       A shopper can pay for purchases by placing their finger on a sensor that reads their fingerprint, linking it to the shopper's bank account or credit card to record the purchase.

2.   Interactive changing room help.

      Using a digital touch screen, a shopper in the changing room of a
      shop can communicate with sales personnel – without having to
      return to the sales floor to search for help.

3.   Smart carts.

      A smart cart incorporates interactive technology via a video screen on
      the front of the shopping cart, enabling customers to locate products,
      access shopping lists, check prices, receive promotions and coupons,
      and scan purchases. The technology also can provide retailers and
      suppliers with rich data on a customer's shopping trip.

4.   3D body scanning.

      A scan of a shopper's body will be used to make recommendations
      about the brands and specific clothes most likely to fit well, or to
      help fit custom-made clothes.

5.   Collaborative product development websites.

      Product developers will encourage consumers to post ideas and
      answer surveys online about new products and how existing
      products can be improved.

6.   Group buying by consumers.

      Shoppers join online collaborative shopping communities to
      aggregate their buying power with other shoppers.

7.   Networked shopping.

      Networked devices in the home – such as refrigerators – will
      monitor what products consumers use, create shopping lists and
      communicate with other devices to arrange deliveries.

8.   Interactive changing room mirror.

      It looks like any other mirror but is actually a high-resolution
      digital screen with a camera that can relay live video and project

holographic images of clothing items so customers can see how they will look in an outfit without trying it on (like a tweet-mirror).

9.   Shopping by mobile phone.

     Shoppers will use mobile devices to place orders and arrange delivery from remote locations.

10. Holographic sales assistant.

     Shoppers will interact with an in-store hologram that can answer questions and facilitate merchandise transactions.

11. Shopping 'social network' websites.

     Shoppers share information about the hottest stores, designers, trends and must-have products – all online. Retailers and suppliers will be able to monitor social networking sites to find out what consumers want and take early action to develop and stock those products.

12. Sales and product information via mobile phone (based on location).

     Shoppers will opt-in to networks that send them text messages about sales, products and retailers that are relevant to the shopper's current location.

Source: TNSglobal.com, May 2008.

All these examples are based on knowing the customers and this is indeed the basis for the future of retailing; knowing the customers and adopting the appropriate approach. Through new technologies it has become increasingly easy to know these customers (see Chapter 5). The implementation is aimed at using this knowledge during the buying moment; stimulating, activating, motivating and facilitating. The consequences for the retail trade will be considerable. In the coming decade this development will lead to a structural change in the retail trade and a change in customer buying behaviour. Technology will play an increasingly important part in physical shopping, as support to individual customers but also overall in shops.

Through this adaptation, physical shopping will remain a clear alternative to Internet shopping. The Internet will gain strength as an infrastructure for online shopping but also for physical shopping. Retailers will be able to develop a multichannel strategy in which they can offer an alternative to the Internet, but it would be much better to incorporate the Internet into their own proposition: in the shop, on the Internet and jointly. This cross-channel strategy is based on the customer and their behaviour. By responding to this effectively during all phases of the buying process there will still be plenty of opportunities. The shop is a physical meeting point to see the products and get personal advice, and sometimes to collect the articles bought on the Internet. In the shop the assistant can help by using the Internet to look at product information, browsing history and special customer data.

New-style Retailing

The structural changes occurring in customer shopping behaviour (shopping 3.0) led to the retail trade having to adapt to the new circumstances. As Darwin observed in the animals on the Galapagos Islands having to mutate depending on the ecostructure, shops will have to adapt to survive.

The circumstances have changed significantly as we have seen. Not only are customers buying differently, they are also using technologies that directly have a negative influence on the competitive strength of the existing retailers. The changes in buying behaviour are not changes based on the same ecostructure because that would mean that customers would still buy in shops – only at different times, on other days or at other local shops. Increased mobility has not led to a structural change either – it is only the place customers go to shop that has changed, not the actual structure of shopping. The rise of Internet shopping has led to a new shop ecostructure, resulting in retailers having to deal with different market circumstances. Customers may now have different buying motives. Understanding these changes is not easy.

It has been presumed that customers only make purchases on the basis of price (the rational customer). Physical shops then face the task of maintaining the same price levels as the Internet shops. However, this is easier said than done: a shop has stock risks and costs for premises and personnel. An Internet shop can operate at with lower overheads and it's even possible to not have any stock at all. Mailing costs are often passed on to the customers. Fighting a competitive battle on the basis of costs is a lost cause for the physical shop.

Customers have to accept that the shop has to charge a higher price but may have other advantages. Of course, not all customers are willing to pay this extra price and they will buy online. They will only return to the shop if they have been disappointed by an online shopping experience.

A recurring aspect of Internet shopping is the fact that purchases are not only made on price. Because of the lower price perception customers are prepared to buy more or to choose a more expensive version of a product. The added value is therefore sought in the intrinsic value perception (I pay less so I can buy something more expensive). However, the role of the salesman is also mentioned as a possible influence on price. A negative reaction from the customer regarding the price will be read by the salesman who may then point out cheaper, but equally good, versions of a product. But the customer may also do this intentionally to see how the salesman reacts. This results in a situation in which customers buy more expensive items when shopping online than in a shop.

Web-shops have a different cost structure to store retailers. This leads to the assumption that selling via the Internet may be cheaper and this is making it hard for existing retailers to compete. However, web-shops have the same buying costs as store retailers, but lower location costs (warehousing), lower staff costs and quite often limited or no stock. These lower overheads put the physical shop at a disadvantage but web-shops have other costs, such as:

- In some cases, the return rate of goods is as high as 50 per cent (fashion): these articles have to be checked and put back on the shelves to be sold again. The 'first' buyers get their money back.

- IT costs might be considerable: websites, procurement systems, warehouse systems, CRM (customer relationship management) marketing systems and communication tools.

- The content on the website has to be renewed on a regular basis: new information, animations, videos and photos of articles. A redesign of the website on a yearly basis is required to keep it looking modern and fresh.

- Customers have to find the site on Internet. Advertising is a major cost for the web-shop, such as bannering, Google adwords and advertising, viral marketing and affiliate marketing. Sometimes online retailers incur costs for advertising on auction sites and comparison sites.

- Finally, offline advertising on TV and in newspapers will lead to a top-of-mind position.

All these costs must be considered! Web-shops, however, maintain competitive prices because they operate in a competitive market. They accept low profit margins per item but aim for high quantity, higher market share and a higher share of customer spend. A high turnover for low margins is the model for web-shops.

New shop variants are emerging on the Internet on the basis of this price perception. Two examples of these variants are brand4friends.de and brandfield.com. The idea is that a small group of people are looking for a discount; members can be recruited who can make use of special offers. This group are regularly informed of offers that remain valid for a short period only. Some offers are only valid for a matter of hours, others for several days. The offers may appear spectacular – capitalizing on being able to reach consumers and on the theory that price is an important aspect of buying. Impulse buys are therefore encouraged.

Being Part of the Search Process

As we have seen, a structural change in the buying process is taking place because the information search is now conducted at home (on the Internet) and no longer in the shop. Retailers therefore have to get involved in the buying process before the time of purchase as by then it is actually too late. Shops can become part of the search process by ensuring that they are easy to find. Search engines like Google seem to be the most appropriate route. By linking the shop name to search terms it's possible to immediately make the association. Sponsored links ensure that you are immediately visible. Another option is to ensure that you are at the top of the selection for a particular search term. Specialist agencies can do this for you. You can also aid the process yourself by placing clear tags in the content of your site, by encouraging site traffic via the use of games, photos and videos, and by placing lots of links to your site from other sites.

There are many steps you can take to make sure you are at the top of the results list in Google:[2]

---

2   www.leerwiki.nl.

- make sure there are sufficient backlinks from the correct websites;

- make sure the correct URL or domain name is used;

- make clever use of the H^1, H$_2$, ^{PRE} and ^{ALT} tags;

- make sure that the document contains sufficient, *correct* keywords;

- make sure your site is listed in link directories;

- make sure you offer quality.

Google is a search engine often used to make searches on the basis of keywords. There must therefore be an association to these keywords. If the search is made by name it is much easier to be top of the list, but users often search by product, as is the case with trading sites and auctions sites. Trading sites were originally websites on which consumers could offer second-hand goods or services. However, shops have discovered these sites and now also offer products through them. From gardening tools to mobility scooters, from cars to clothing, more and more shops can be found selling their wares amidst the second-hand items offered by private individuals. Consumers can see the price difference for themselves and visit the physical shop. Suddenly, the shop has become appealing to people outside the local area. My hairdresser now has customers from all over the country because he offers hair care and anti-hair loss products online. For the physical shops it's important to use sites with a lot of traffic. The difference between trading sites and search engines in the eyes of the Internet user is the intention behind the search. Google is used to search for information, while a concrete buying intention is the motive for searching on an auction or trading site.

Another development on the Internet that is significant for retailers is the increasing collaboration between suppliers: the convergence and concentration development. More and more parties are getting together in order to be able to offer a total collection on the basis of a search key word. One example of this is Internet shopping centres (digicities) where retailers from the same town or city get together on the same site. They then offer a wide range of services with the location as the distinguishing feature.

As a result of these sites the physical shops can be found faster and the customer is motivated to go to the shopping centre after all. Also, there is an increasing degree of collaboration between retailers, allowing the customer to make a better choice based upon comparision sites. Customers compare products on such comparison sites so it's important to be listed on these too. Obviously the comparison criteria should be verified accurately. A negative comparison is always negative for sales. This comparison is an important component of the new buying process. It seems only logical, therefore, that new applications should emerge for comparison. This can be done through the aforementioned sites and also by searching the Internet yourself. Google was the most appropriate medium for this but, because of the volume of information, is still not quite the right medium. Seventy per cent of people searching don't look any further than the first page. The recent Microsoft development, in which a new search machine was launched to make this comparison easier, suits shopping 3.0.

MICROSOFT'S NEW SEARCH ENGINE AT BING.COM HELPS PEOPLE MAKE BETTER DECISIONS

Decision Engine goes beyond search to help customers deal with information overload.

REDMOND, Wash. — May 28, 2009 — Microsoft Corp. today unveiled Bing, a new Decision Engine and consumer brand, providing customers with a first step in moving beyond search to help make faster, more informed decisions. Bing is specifically designed to build on the benefits of today's search engines but begins to move beyond this experience with a new approach to user experience and intuitive tools to help customers make better decisions, focusing initially on four key vertical areas: making a purchase decision, planning a trip, researching a health condition or finding a local business. The result of this new approach is an important beginning for a new and more powerful kind of search service, which Microsoft is calling a Decision Engine, designed to empower people to gain insight and knowledge from the Web, moving more quickly to important decisions. The new service, located at http:// www.Bing.com, will begin to roll out over the coming days and will be fully deployed worldwide on Wednesday, June 3. The explosive growth of online content has continued unabated, and Bing was developed as a tool to help people more easily navigate through the information overload that has come to characterize many of today's search experiences. Results from a custom comScore Inc. study across core search engines show that as many as 30 percent of searches are abandoned without a satisfactory result. The data also showed that approximately two-

thirds of the remaining searches required a refinement or requery on the search results page. 'Today, search engines do a decent job of helping people navigate the Web and find information, but they don't do a very good job of enabling people to use the information they find,' said Steve Ballmer, Microsoft CEO. 'When we set out to build Bing, we grounded ourselves in a deep understanding of how people really want to use the Web. Bing is an important first step forward in our long-term effort to deliver innovations in the search that enable people to find information quickly and use the information they've found to accomplish tasks and make smart decisions.'

Source: www.microsoft.com.

Because of this, the competition between Microsoft and Google is tougher than ever. Microsoft has held a dominant position in PC software since the 1980s, mainly due to the Windows operating system. Many other programs such as Word and PowerPoint were introduced for PC users on the basis of this system. The office environment was actually a Microsoft environment. After a hesitant start with the Internet, Internet Explorer was added in 1995; this was a browser linked directly to Windows. Thanks to this link Explorer attained a market share of almost 100 per cent, although this has since changed. In the last couple of years there has been increasing pressure to undo this automatic link and to sell the browser as a separate program. This link was removed mainly under pressure from the EU. At the same time other browsers appeared that became increasingly popular, with Firefox as the leader and Safari the popular choice with Apple computer users.

Web Statistics and Trends

Statistics provide important information. From the statistics below (Table 4.1), you can see that Internet Explorer and Firefox are the most common browsers.

Further to this, Google has entered into competition with Microsoft in other areas. Google firstly launched a rival to Word (Google Docs), followed by a browser (Chrome) and then a new operating system for netbooks. With these products, Google aims to be a dominant force on the Internet and also on PCs. The netbook is a logical first step in this because they are linked to the Internet. Microsoft also wants to supply the operating system for netbooks with Windows 7. This battle has resulted in Microsoft wanting to be more

Table 4.1   Browser statistics month by month (%)

2010	IE8	IE7	IE6	Firefox	Chrome	Safari	Opera
April	16.2%	9.3%	7.9%	46.4%	13.6%	3.7%	2.2%
March	15.3%	10.7%	8.9%	46.2%	12.3%	3.7%	2.2%
February	14.7%	11.0%	9.6%	46.5%	11.6%	3.8%	2.1%
January	14.3%	11.7%	10.2%	46.3%	10.8%	3.7%	2.2%
2009	IE8	IE7	IE6	Firefox	Chrome	Safari	Opera
December	13.5%	12.8%	10.9%	46.4%	9.8%	3.6%	2.3%
November							

Source: Adapted from W3Schools.com.

dominant on the Internet. However, its own MSN portal, with a browser, news facility, mail (hotmail) and messenger has not yet had the success Microsoft had hoped for. In 2009, Microsoft made two significant Internet-based developments: a collaboration with Yahoo and the introduction of the search engine Bing. This combination should form a strong counterweight to Google.

> *Microsoft and Yahoo yesterday concluded an agreement for the next ten years. The deal means that Yahoo will make use of Bing, the brand new Microsoft search engine, for all searches on its websites. In turn, Yahoo will deal with the global sales of advertisements to large companies, for both Yahoo itself and for Microsoft. Smaller companies will continue to use Microsoft Ad Center.*

Source: Nieuwsvoorziening, 28 July 2009.

One of the most important forthcoming developments is the enhancement of the portal function. It is important to get traffic and most popular sites will link on to other sites (affiliates). A good example is a portal that covers a certain topic and gives links to relevant sites. E-commerce will become much simpler for customers as a result and the development of Internet shopping centres is stimulated by this. Bing is not just a search engine that searches for terms – like Google – it is more. On the basis of the search term, companies can also buy an entry on Bing, ensuring a prominent result to a relevant search. This entry can be straightforward: beauty salon under beauty salons or a car brand from the search term 'cars', but with Bing it can also be associative: for example, the search term 'books Portugal' could also show hotels in Portugal or Portuguese wine. In fact this creates a search association which users should experience as logical. Searches can also be made on the basis of these associations. With the search term 'car', links can also be offered to accessories, car shows or self-drive holidays. Other links are then shown based on associations. From this perspective, the deal between Yahoo and Microsoft could be the forerunner of a new use of Internet search engines and could capitalize on associative customer behaviour.

Microsoft focuses on four areas: making a buying decision, making a travel plan, health surveys and finding a local business or shop. It is therefore responding directly to shopping 3.0 and the new style of retailing. Both are concerned with the combination of the Internet and the physical shop but are also based on customer behaviour. This will also push retailers into creating their own website. Retailers need to be found on the Internet and the search term will direct customers to their shop. Do you intend to sell on the Internet or to use the Internet for reference purposes only? Your own website, which really is essential, should immediately answer the customer's need for information and demonstrate the focus of the shop.

The purpose of the website has to be clear. In its most elementary form it is an information site giving the shop opening times and contact details. A fully-fledged Internet strategy is also needed – it's not a good choice to simply deal with the online orders as a sideline – that would mean competing against all those professional Internet retailers, an uneven fight! Play a home game and compete, on your own strengths, in the shop. For physical shops the Internet is a support for shopping 3.0, not a new buying medium.

'New retailing' is the philosophy that customers are buying differently and have to be supported in the buying process. It's no longer sufficient for a shop to be open at regular times and advertise in the local paper. The very least the new approach requires is a good listing on the Internet with contact details, a listing among other relevant suppliers and sites and marketplaces like eBay. Shops can only survive by capitalizing on the new buying and shopping behaviours of customers. New retailing in this form is in effect a forerunner of cross-channel retailing, in which the technology is integrated in the retail sector (see Figure 4.6).

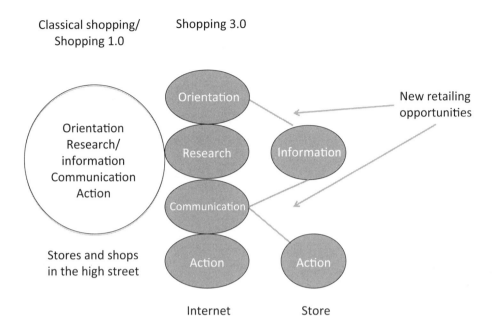

Figure 4.6   A combination of virtual reality and physical shopping

This will be discussed in the next chapter.

TOUCH-SCREEN SELFRIDGES WINDOW DISPLAYS ALLOW SHOPPERS TO TRY ON VIRTUAL 3D WATCHES

Selfridges has unveiled two touch-screen window displays which will allow shoppers to 'try on' virtual 3D watches without even entering the store.

Passers-by outside the Oxford Street store will be handed paper wristbands which, when shown to a camera built into the display, will allow them to view an image of themselves 'wearing' any watch they select on the touch-screen.

The 'virtual watch' is created by real-time light-reflecting technology that allows the consumer to interact with the design by twisting their wrist for a 360 degree view.

Shoppers will be able to 'try on' 28 different watches from the Touch collection by the Swiss watch maker Tissot, and can also experiment with different dials and straps.

Each watch will show the correct time and date and shoppers will also be able to try their touch-screen functions such as compasses and thermometers.

Lynne Murray, Brand Director for Holition, which designed the 3D technology, said: 'We are excited to be part of such a step-change in the luxury watch market's approach to its customer relationship.'

'Using fully immersive augmented reality, Holition is enabling upmarket brands to remain cutting edge and experience a much higher level of consumer engagement with the product.'

The paper wristbands will be handed out for free outside the flagship Oxford Street Selfridges store from 9am until 9pm for two weeks from Thursday.

Source: Daily Telegraph, 13 May 2010.

Summary

- Use the Internet to support customers in the buying process. An order doesn't even have to be placed, providing information is often sufficient for the physical retailer. If something is sold make sure you offer specific products with added value for the customer. Be rational; think from the customer's perspective.

- Web retailers have to add more emotion. Rational shopping is certainly easy, but not fun. Make sure you use a good colour scheme, clear navigation and easily recognized contact details. Work with attractive film clips and animations (that only run when clicked on).

- Take advantage of the speed of the medium, which means rapid replies, fast deliveries and personal service.

- Make sure you can be found on the Internet, on Google, on eBay and on portals.

- Make your site attractive and fun featuring news, cool clips, photos and interaction. Encourage customer involvement in the site (guestbook or photo album).

- Offer trust through the return policy: Money back guarantee, no questions asked!

In 2015 the retailing landscape will have transformed completely. Although a lot of the technologies around at the moment will be key to driving this change, they will have evolved considerably. For shoppers, the look and feel of shopping will continue to change as many existing retail concepts meet the end of their shelf life. Retail businesses will have to innovate continuously as an increasingly digital environment gives shoppers dramatic new choices. Consumer products manufacturers will need to respond to these trends and embrace new assumptions. These changes reflect many trends. The Baby Boom generation – which has dominated retail thinking for decades – will be turning 70 and the baton will be passed to Generation Y. Technology will become increasingly available. Shoppers will interact with retailers and suppliers more than ever before, with online capabilities and communities playing a bigger and bigger role in the relationship.

The new future is unfolding now; this report provides a glimpse of what's in store for shoppers, for retailers, and for the manufacturers who create the myriad of consumer products we buy every day.

The Web is shaping up to be one of retail's bright spots this holiday season, thanks in part to a new take on an old-fashioned retail idea: good service.

At a time when traditional retailers are being ultra conservative, many Web sites have been spending to make shipping times faster, consumer-generated reviews better, and to offer new features such as online layaways. Amazon.com Inc. is rolling out more 'frustration-free' packages that replace hard-to-open plastic clamshells; eBay Inc. is highlighting merchants with the best ratings; and Sears Holdings Corp. is launching online layaway.

Source: Wall Street Journal, 28 October 2009.

5

Technology Makes Buying Easy: Integrating Bricks and Mortar with the Internet

Technology makes buying easy. The time when a retailer added up the bill on a piece of paper has long gone. The electronic cash till came into use on a massive scale in the 1950s, followed by all sorts of computerization in the 1960s and 1970s (administrative computerization). In the 1980s and 1990s, till transactions (barcodes) and purchasing also became computerized and computers were used to facilitate customer relations – communication became targeted and personalized. Databases holding customer details, loyalty systems like Airmiles and, ultimately, the Internet ensured there was an integrated process from the manufacturer via the shop to the consumer.

These developments all fitted into the vision of that time – supply oriented with the customer as the last link. But all that was about to change, initiated by the customers themselves. As we have seen in previous chapters, the customer buying process is becoming increasingly dominant within the retail sector, with choice in both the range and the media, and the connection with the customer is becoming more and more important. Customers have become intangible; they show initiative and shift their boundaries (no longer bound to shopping locally, customers can shop wherever they choose – as long as they understand the language being used by the website and feel an affinity to it).

Computerization in shops, aimed at making the shop efficient as a distribution point, is now being replaced by computerization that supports the shopping process. This should place the key focus on the buying process, as a result of integration with the Internet for example, or a link on Google, or entry via a portal. This change, from supply to demand and from selling to buying, presents a major challenge for shops.

The need to computerize is also intensified by the increasing pressure on returns, due to shopping 3.0 on one hand and the recession on the other which, in turn, puts pressure on profit margins. This means that the need for greater efficiency in sales is felt by the management of retail companies, which leads to:

- a need for better, up-to-date management information;

- a need to make the processes, such as purchasing and stock management, efficient and to ensure that there is neither over- nor under-stocking;

- the need for effective communications with customers;

- natural anticipation of and response to the buying process, in which the Internet plays an important role.

Computerization in the retail sector is very strongly oriented towards the existing processes and the existing methods of working, which results in the supply being central and not the customer. Computerization within the existing processes of a shop is dominated by traditional shop computerization, enterprise resource planning (ERP) systems and administrative systems. Purchasing can be done traditionally; the stock is registered on the basis of a barcode and the till sales are linked to the stock and to the financial administration. The changes that are now taking place in the retail sector have a lot to do with the new technological possibilities that are based on recognition and registration of customers (tracking and tracing) and the role that the Internet plays for both the shop and for customers. In this switchover the focus changes from supply to demand. Computerization also has to be modified to deal with this and therefore more focused on the customer and customer behaviour than on the supply: a shift of focus from transactions to demand. In fact, the focus shifts from selling to supporting the buying process.

Recognition at Product Level

In recent decades the barcode has become an integrated component of a product. With the unique number combination – the international article number (EAN), sales at item level could be better registered, the article stock could be more easily determined and the purchasing process optimized. Stocktaking to determine what has to be bought in is no longer necessary; this is now a computerized process. New offerings can be developed as a result of intense collaboration between a supplier, manufacturer, importer or wholesaler. These may be new solutions such as customer-based pricing and auction sites. New methods of stock control means that stock can become the joint responsibility of the stock and a third party (for example, the supplier or manufacturer) or solely the responsibility of the third party. This enables the retailer to focus entirely on customer contact and the relationship with the market. The shop's financing needs can also be reduced as stocks are on consignment and not the property of the retailer but of the supplier. Based on sales, stocks can be replenished and the other party paid. Consignation is a traditional form of transaction where payment is made depending on what is drawn from the stock. The retailer therefore only pays upon the sale of the articles. This leads to a lower investment and lower costs. This has become a necessity as a result of the price differences between physical and online stores.

Computerization has led to changes because the third party now has direct insight into stock levels. This is made possible by linking the till registration to the stock registration – the other party can decide to restock (and effect settlement with the shop). This way of sharing responsibilities (collaboration), in which one party ensures that sales are good and the other that stocks are good, is also known as VMI (vendor-managed inventory). If fair agreements are made about stock levels and the speed of delivery, each party can apply their own competencies.

Having direct insight into the stock levels enables the third party, often the manufacturer, sometimes a wholesaler or distributor, to keep in touch with the market on a daily basis. The cost levels for the shop fall, resulting in a better chance of competing with Internet stores.

This creates an advantageous situation and mutual dependence for both parties. Two additional developments stimulate this approach: the application of RFID chips and integration with the Internet.

The Radio Frequency Identification Chip

The RFID chip makes it easier to track items, both at article level and/or pallet level. Goods movements can be mapped out and their location directly monitored. This can be done by the supplier, but also by the retailer. Goods in transit can also be tracked this way. An additional benefit is that a record can be placed on the chip allowing clear monitoring of the shipment date, transportation time and transportation conditions. By using the memory on the chip, extra product information can also be stored, such as price, article number, ingredients, date and place of manufacture, and the best before/ sell by date. An RFID chip attached to an article can also be used for theft prevention: an alarm sounds if the item leaves its designated areas and passes a gate or signal. The chips therefore perform several functions for the retailer: an administrative function for stock control, a location indicator for tracking and tracing, a till transaction function and a theft prevention function.

> *These tags can be 'active', 'semi-active/semi-passive' or 'passive'. Active RFID tags are powered by a battery and can be read and written with a 'remote transceiver' also called a 'reader', which sends and receives radio waves with an antenna. Active tags usually transmit their ID intermittently; semi-active tags only transmit their signal once it has been activated by the reader. Passive RFID tags have no power supply and transmit an answer by transforming the energy of the radio waves transmitted by the reader.*

Source: Wikipedia on RFID.

In addition to a chip at article level, the chip can also be applied at a personal level. It is possible to track articles (or containers) at article level, which enables enhanced stock registration, but also means that new concepts like VMI can be executed better. At a personal level this chip enables identification, so that new services can be offered to customers in the shop. One example of this is a chip in a mobile phone, which creates a unique personal identification that can be the basis of, for example, a pay function. A recent test revealed that users were 100 per cent satisfied with this integrated application (pay via your telephone). The combination of chip and telephone will ultimately replace plastic cards. The chip is then a means of identification, and as such can be a basis for the registration of people in various systems, such as pay systems, customer programmes and access systems. The person is identified by the chip, sometimes in combination with another identifying mark such as a pin code or iris scan.

> *NFC: Near Field Communications is a clever form of RFID. Where RFID is applied primarily for the storage and one-way transmission of data, NFC uses two-way communication and can receive and process*

signals. Philips developed the NFC technique together with Sony. Among other applications, NFC will be used in mobile phones as a way of paying and in ticket systems. The collaboration with Nokia was important for the ultimate possibilities for use in telephones.

*Source:*Wikipedia.nl on NFC (Near Field Communication).

The use of the RFID chip is actually important to the retail sector. The combination of chip and reader makes it possible to provide extra services like NFC. This means that customers can be tracked and informed during the buying process. This form of NFC in combination with narrowcasting – direct video – is the ultimate in customer contact support. The chip is then a customer card which also includes a profile of the customer. Extra buying support can be given on the basis of this profile. Linking with a reader at the till, for example, makes it possible to register information on the chip, but also to use that information as an extra form of communication, loyalty points, as a part of a saving programme, but also to offer discounts on the basis of historic buying behaviour, to recommend buying (or receiving) accessories. The extra information, which comes available more or less automatically at customer level, must become part of the buying experience. The information can be stored on a chip (in the customer card or mobile phone) and is therefore owned by the customer.

Customer information can also be stored in a central system belonging to the retailer. The customer's chip has a customer number only; this chip then activates the retailer's database. A system at the till is a classic example of this: the items sold are then registered to the customer number, as already happens with a supermarket loyalty card and the Airmiles card. This information can also be accessed in the shop as part of an information pillar, where the customer uses their chip to activate a system which then tells them whether there are any special offers or discounts they are entitled to, and so on. The customer enjoys this and sees it as a reason to visit the shop: what do they have for me now?

Another application is narrowcasting – direct video; this makes use of a screen (or information pillar) located in the shop that is activated by the customer. This can be done actively by holding the pass or telephone in front of a reader, but it could also be done passively when the customer with the chip comes near the screen. What then appears on the screen are messages specifically aimed at this customer. The customer can also enter questions (interact) about the most recent purchases, a suggested purchase or about accessories or stocks. The screen takes over some of the sales assistant's dialogue (and communications) with the customer. This application is based on an RFID chip linked to a customer card. However, the current application of narrowcasting is mostly still generic. The screens scroll continuously or are activated by the people who are walking in its vicinity. The information provided is clearly offer oriented, but can also be guided by general triggers, such as the weather, product information or purchase suggestions. This could be used to entertain people waiting in a queue at the checkout, for example. McDonald's make use of this, with the narrowcasting information being dependent on the time of day, the length of the queue and the outside temperature (McFlurry or Big Mac?). With personally initiated narrowcasting (via the RFID chip), identification, historic buying behaviour and customer relationship are utilized. This enables personal messages or buying suggestions. The promotion of other items is also a possibility, where suggestions are given for alternative or matching items. The combination of the personally-linked chip and the article chip in the fitting room springs to mind. In this case, a customer trying on certain products could receive information about the product, what other sizes are in stock, but could also see accessories that would go well with it. The mirror is then both reader and screen. While you look in the mirror to see what the item looks like, other suggestions are also immediately shown, as well as where these accessories are to be found in the shop. In the privacy of the fitting room the customer can calmly consider the possible purchase and decide what to buy.

As described in Chapter 1, contact with the sales assistant leads to a personal interaction but also to a dialogue about the price. On the Internet this is a different sort of buying experience, because customers can choose and decide for themselves if they want to. The described development of narrowcasting, and the application in the fitting room, constitute a combination of buying behaviour on the Internet and buying behaviour in the shop. In the shop, a product is sought and no suggestions given or associations made – features that are a powerful feature of the Internet buying process. With technology allowing these functions in a shop – freedom of choice, combination buying suggestions and the fact that customers can take the items with them straight away – it is likely that the customer's overall spend will increase. The buying experience will be enhanced and the customer perceives that they are being treated in a more personal manner. The physical shop will gain strength from this. This use of RFID on articles and on the personally-linked card (or telephone) will be an important development within the retail sector, a support to shopping 3.0.

SELEXYZ/BOEKHANDELSGROEP NEDERLAND

In the Selexyz (Boekhandels Groep Nederland) shops in Almere and Maastricht all books have RFID tags. The books that Selexyz orders from the Centraal Boekhuis are fitted with a passive RFID tag. The order is scanned on arrival with a tunnel scanner. Using this means the box doesn't have to be opened to check whether the order is correct and complete. This not only ensures that Selexyz' logistic process is optimized but also that customers can know immediately whether the book they want is in stock. At a kiosk customers can see for themselves in which bookcase they can find the book of their choice. Selexyz intends to fit all their shops with RFID technology.

Realized through: Progress, Capturetech, Boekhandelsgroep Nederland (Selexyz)

Source: RFID Platform Nederland.

Integration with the Internet

Integration with the Internet makes it possible to create a direct link to another database system. Computer systems can therefore be linked to each other, for example those of the shop and the supplier. Signals can be passed on, on the basis of triggers, which are necessary for the logistic process; this could be in relation to minimum stock levels, out of stock situations or articles that are in transit (delivery times), and the aforementioned VMI concept.

A particular development within computerization presupposes the linking of computer systems and information sources (for instance, grid computing and cloud computing). Consequently, it's possible to provide better support for functions and to avoid an overlap in information. Different parties can therefore use a central computer system for separate business functions, and information can be stored once somewhere and be accessible through a network to different systems or for different functions.

The shop registers its stock, which automatically triggers an order, which is then delivered by the supplier. Both can use the same system, thus creating transparency. Collaboration at a functional level may also be considered. The retail sector is strong in maintaining contact with the market and customers while a supplier's strength lies in the delivery of goods. The Internet is a relatively new medium for the retail trade; it distorts the basic processes in the shop because customers are now better informed and are aware of what's for sale. Through close collaboration between the shop and a supplier, an Internet site can be developed which provides an ordering function, in effect a normal e-shop under the name of the shop. The external party can then deal with the orders so that the shop only receives the proceeds of the sales and has no further worries about the delivery of items. Customers receive the ordered items from the shop. The follow-up of the order can be provided directly by a distributor or a manufacturer, but it's also possible to contract the delivery out to a specialized company.

> *Docdata processes over a million and a half transactions each month for its customers in The Netherlands and in the UK (like eBay). Transactions include: the booking of an order, the processing of a payment, the dispatching of an order and the handling of a return shipment. The company is active with its Internet services in the Netherlands, Germany and the United Kingdom.*

Source: FD.nl, 28 July 2009.

In this way, storage and logistics service companies look after the operations side for various Internet suppliers. The e-retailer can concentrate fully on their relationship with the market, the product range and the communications with customers. The orders are handled by the service company, including packing, invoicing, dispatch and transport to the logistics service, on behalf of and under the name of the shop. Through this collaboration of specialisms there is greater competitive power, more specific expertise and greater efficiency. It's precisely this specialization that signifies a growing maturity of the Internet (Adam Smith stated that specialization is the source of welfare). The splitting of customer contact and delivery is a remarkable development; it leads to collaboration between the suppliers and to a mutual interdependence. Different rules apply on the Internet to those in a physical shop; the customer is the key focus for Internet shops. Customers buy on the Internet; in shops things are sold!

Along with the more or less static information provided by an Internet shop, a sales incentive should also be given; there should be impulses to go to other pages and to buy items. This can be done with banners, images, links or information; in-text links are especially effective.

In addition, purchasing and payment must be easy and the customer must be able to see the status of the order immediately. The most important elements of a web-shop are convenience and reduction of uncertainty, together with a personal approach.

The retail store will change from a distribution function to a customer service point, supported by the supplier (see Figure 5.1).

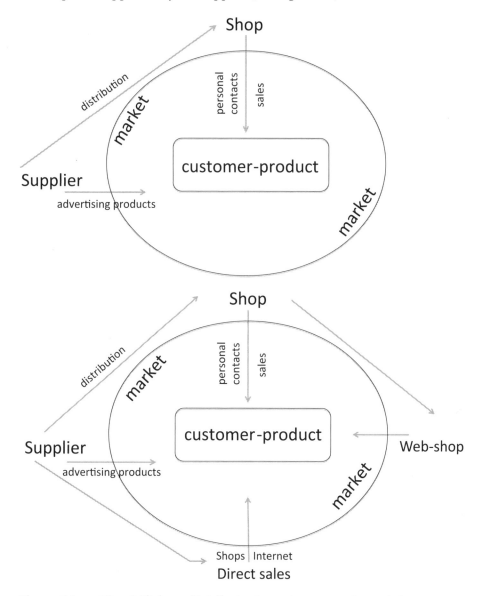

Figure 5.1   The shift from distributor to customer service point

Multichannel

The single-channel approach demands that you excel in one channel and make use of the competitive strength that applies to it; with a multichannel approach you have to excel in several channels, such as a physical shop and on the Internet. There is, for example, plenty of experience in the physical shop, which is optimized by the implementation of computerization and the know-how of the founder. Location and product range are dominant but customer knowledge is often lacking.

This is about interaction, professional know-how and the right moment. On the Internet it is possible to register customer behaviour. Many analysis systems make customer behaviour profiles in order to gain more knowledge about the buying pattern and also of the individual customer. This enables purchasing suggestions to be made and the projection of future buying behaviour is possible on the basis of historic behaviour and associations. The individual customer is central in Internet retailing, whilst in the physical retail sector the product takes the central position (customer-based versus transaction-based).

It is difficult for an organization to have a good multichannel strategy: it means having to fight on several fronts, against companies that are specifically focused on that one channel (the pure players). This is not only problematic; it also leads to disappointment amongst customers. If you already know a certain retailer in the physical world, you expect the same feeling and the same approach (in your perception) on the Internet and vice versa of course. This is easier said than done. There is often a difference in approach and a difference in experience; the computer systems of the shop and the Internet site are rarely linked to each other. As a result, a customer from the shop may not be recognized on the Internet, not get suggestions and not have the feeling that they are really recognized. In the shop it's about transactions and the personal contact. This may be perceived by the customer as a breach of trust and may, in a best case scenario, lead to separate buying processes where purchases are made in different stores online to the physical world.

Such findings confirm that the online shopping channel is firmly embedded in the public consciousness, and that e-tailers are doing things right and producing satisfied customers. Perhaps more important is the evidence that even in difficult economic times, shoppers care about more than just price – two-thirds of respondents in the Likemind survey said they would be turned off of making a purchase by poor service – and are looking at the full picture of what retailers can provide.

'Online merchants need to look beyond price and convenience,' said eMarketer Senior Analyst Karin von Abrams. 'These have been key drivers of online shopping growth in the past, along with the rising number of consumers using the Internet and having positive experiences online.'

'But online stores will increasingly be defined and differentiated by their standards of service – especially when the overall rate of growth is slowing,' she said.

Improving customer service also gives e-tailers the opportunity to appeal to customer segments that may have been overlooked. Consumers who particularly value conscientious, reliable service typically include those with higher incomes and older people whose expectations of service were formed before the age of the Web.

Likemind said the respondents most likely to consider service better online were those ages 55 and older, many of whom have not yet adopted online shopping with the zeal of younger groups.

Source: www.emarketer.com.

It is not the case that a successful shop in the physical world will automatically be a success on the Internet. It's quite possible, of course, but there needs to be clear customer recognition in the shop – such as that which occurs on the Internet – and there should be emotion on the Internet – such as is possible in the shop. The services should at least be equal. Matching perceptions is a difficult task. Efforts are made to combine the advantages of the one channel with the other channel and, to a certain degree, these succeed. Customers become used to the workings of a particular channel and would like to see the same in another channel. On the Internet a customer is recognized from their login data, thus enabling personal support. But why should an identical strategy be conducted on both channels? It's really more logical to be leading on one channel and for the other channel to be supporting. If the shop is leading then support functionality can be offered via the Internet. The John Lewis chain of stores is an example of this. The shops are the leading channel, as a result of the large brand confidence and the affinity customers have with the store. The ordering process is very desirable – items can be ordered online and either collected in-store or delivered to the customer's home. The Internet channel is closely intertwined with the shop formula and is based on customer requirements and the buying process.

> If you can't wait in for your delivery, or you're looking for a quick and convenient way to get your hands on your latest purchase, our new Click & collect service could be just what you're looking for.
>
> It's a free service, no matter what the value of your order, and it's available for most items sold on our website. It's simple – just order before 7pm today and pick up from your chosen shop's collection point from 2pm tomorrow. If you're not able to pick up your item the next day, don't worry, we'll keep it for you for 7 days.
>
> This service guarantees that your order will be in stock at your chosen shop, as we'll despatch it overnight. We're also trialling the service at selected Waitrose branches.
>
> For your security, if we have your mobile phone number, we'll send you a text message to let you know your goods are ready for collection from your chosen shop. You'll need to save the text, and bring your phone with you to show it as proof of purchase, along with some ID. Otherwise, you'll just need to bring along a printout of your order receipt or confirmation email, plus proof of ID.

Source: Johnlewis.com.

Another example is Diako Easyfit. This company supports slimming processes by supplying calorie-controlled, high protein and vitamin meals. The German branch has implemented a combination of an Internet shop and a physical contact point. In the large department stores (such as Karstad) there is a shop-in-shop concept, where Diako Easyfit leases a few square metres. Here the customer can contact a dietician for advice and can also collect their orders, if preferred. Large department stores have been chosen specially as meeting points because most women do actually visit these places, and there's then no barrier to entering a shop. It's precisely this combination of physical service and support of dietary wishes with the option of collecting the balanced meals that gives Diako Easyfit that extra trust. Of course it's possible to do everything via the Internet – both the orders and the service. Customers can choose for themselves; it's the physical contact point that contributes to trust, but it is supportive of the Internet proposition.

Customer Relationship Marketing and the Internet

The cross-channel approach is a good alternative for existing (large) retail stores; support can consequently be given on the basis of individual buying processes. This does, of course, demand a specific approach from computerization. A good back office is organized from the shop, an ERP system registers what happens. Over the last decade, some stores have also implemented a CRM system. CRM is a widely implemented strategy for managing and nurturing a company's interactions with customers, clients and sales prospects. It involves using technology to organize, automate and synchronize business processes – principally sales activities, but also those for marketing customer service and technical support. The overall goals are to find, attract and win new customers, nurture and retain those the company already has, stimulate former customers back and reduce the costs of marketing and client service. When an implementation is effective, people, processes and technology work in synergy to increase profitability, and reduce operational costs.

These systems stem from the supply-oriented approach. CRM is usually an extra functionality within the ERP systems (such as SAP, Oracle and Microsoft). The core is the ERP systems. The CRM systems register customer data and enable direct communication: these systems are often used in call centres and customer contact centres to register correspondence between the customers and the retailer. It is supportive of the communication process and ensures efficient contacts. These systems are also used for efficient communication through other media: mailings, outbound telemarketing and e-mails. This makes it possible to execute individually oriented communications on a mass scale.

On the basis of the historic developments described in Chapter 3, this mass scale is based on collective individuality within the supply and sales paradigm. These CRM systems may not always be linked to transaction systems. As a result of this it is not always possible to define customer values and to communicate on this. The CRM system consists of a database holding customer data and a communication module.

Preferred shopping experience: Over 75 percent of shoppers cited that they prefer shopping 'Online to Store' followed by 'Store to Online' (7+

percent) and 'Online to Call Center' (3+ percent) across all product categories – these combinations were nearly identical for US and UK consumers. Based on average basket size, consumers in the US spent the most on purchases made between the 'Online to Call Center' channels. On the flip side, consumers in the UK spent the most between the 'Online to Mobile' segments.

Profile of multi-channel shopper: In the US, the age group with the greatest percentage of multi-channel shoppers (those who are defined by shopping once a month or more) is 18–24 years; in the UK, core multi-channel shoppers are slightly older between 25–34 years.

Switching loyalties between channels and retailers: Between 46–50 percent of all shoppers in the US and the UK admitted to switching loyalties to retailers as they shopped across different channels. Overall, most consumers cited price as their primary motivation for change, followed by convenience and product availability.

Source: www.risnews.com, 10 July 2008.

The fact that communications are personal does not necessarily indicate that an organization is customer oriented. This limitation occurs in the world of the physical retailer but also happens with Internet retailers, which seems strange as on the Internet all data is automatically recorded; indeed, this is part of the core process. The CRM module has become part of the basic process but that often leads to a process-oriented approach.

Buying suggestions generated by Internet shops are usually based on the previously purchased items (as is the case on Amazon.com). It is advantageous to include more individual behavioural criteria in this so that a match with other buyers with similar behaviour is possible. But is this then personal? This process applies a rigid approach from within the system, in which the product is the basis and not the behaviour. These associations are also transaction based and not supportive of a relationship. The association is therefore not intuitive but entirely process driven, based on previous product purchases. The best buying suggestions are based on historic behaviour, customer profiles and article characteristics, and compared with similar buying behaviour of other customers (see Figure 5.2).

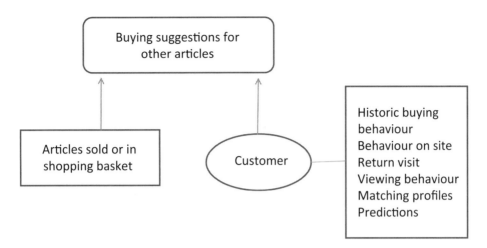

Figure 5.2   Generating buying suggestions based on customer profiles

An intuitive application is based on behavioural characteristics, in which the time of day, landing page, length of time on the site, articles viewed and articles bought are placed in a certain pattern, which in turn will lead to the creation of customer profiles that can be matched. This is certainly not the case here but technology does make it possible. Personalization of the website, tailored personal offers and triggered response are possibilities that could be integrated into the buying process. The triggers and the personalization are based on events. These are the actual contact moments on the website or in the shop. These events should lead to communications that correspond precisely with the moment and the customer. It is this convergence of technology and its adoption by customers that will be important to the relationship with customers in the coming Internet period (2008–2020).[1]

Nowadays, every self-respecting supplier offers their customers the possibility of personalizing websites with a 'My homepage' option. Up to now the services behind this were often restricted to modifying personal details, for example, or submitting meter readings. But the turning point is close and it is getting closer because a technological change is also taking place; namely the development, during the credit crisis, of the convergence of infrastructures such as cable, mobile phone and satellite, and the integration of data: aptly referred to as 'unified communications'.

These two effects, the personalization of services and the convergence of infrastructures and data, will strengthen each other in the coming years. The

---

1   Complex event processing is based upon algorithms to decide the message for the customer.

consumer will see that they can feel connected anytime, anywhere and will increasingly demand this of their service providers. The business world will have no choice but to invest. The outcome of this crisis: a Martini-style world in which information about everything and everyone is available 'any time, any place, anywhere'.

The conclusion, therefore, is that a company not only needs to have a connectivity strategy but also needs to fix two other matters:

1.   Continuous analysis of customers and their buying behaviour. Understanding what customers respond to. Companies need to be able to profile customers and set up personalized sales strategies; not just once but continuously. This therefore demands advanced analysis software. It's not for nothing that there have been takeovers in this sector in recent years by various parties like SAP (Business Objects) and IBM (SPSS).

2.   Integrating sense and response solutions into the primary process. It is therefore imperative to set up a sales system in which all sales conditions for each customer can be individually monitored in real time in order to continuously define the best sales strategies. This requires powerful engines that can recognize relevant situations for sales from these large data flows in real time and can take action upon them. The existing database-oriented technologies are often not fast enough to do this. The technology that is generally accepted as making the above possible is called Complex Event Processing.

Customer Analysis as Part of the Buying Process

This event-based communication is part of a customer analysis strategy. With event-based communications the moment and the customer behaviour are central, but in terms of the operational management, analyses are also needed at a higher aggregation level. Indeed, it is the analysis of what happens within the company, the departments and in relation to the customers that must serve as the basis for the company strategy. Convergence of systems is important here too. All the data produced by the computerization system, process control, department computerization, ERP and CRM must be integrated and interpreted. This demands powerful analysis systems. It's not so strange, therefore, that traditional computerization companies are integrating this analysis software into their own systems. Collaborations between suppliers are increasingly closer.

TAKEOVER SPSS IS A CLEVER MOVE BY IBM

It's not actually so surprising that IBM took over SPSS, one of the few independent suppliers of predictive analysis software. That's the view of the Computable panel Business Intelligence (BI). 'A clever move by IBM,' according to Mathijs Kreugel of VLC. The ICT company wants to present itself on the analytics market and with the takeover can profit from synergy advantages.

The software giant took over SPSS for 1.2 billion dollars. At the end of 2007 the company also took over BI supplier Cognos. That was IBM's first major move in the business intelligence market. IBM aims to secure a leading position in the BI and analytics market and is looking to present itself as a supplier of a complete value proposition, Ricardo Passchier of BPM supplier IDS Scheer explained.

Source: www.computable.nl.

In the application field of the Internet we have seen collaboration between Microsoft and Yahoo; integrating the new search engine Bing into Yahoo. More advertisers can also be secured. Integration is also taking place within the software companies, where it is no longer sufficient to computerize operating processes or company functions. Integration of ERP and CRM applications has already taken place. In this context, for example, Oracle bought out CRM software market leader Siebel and has integrated Siebel into its own applications. Microsoft also has various CRM applications, such as Navision, and SAP has integrated its own CRM program.

Now that the focus has again become knowledge of customers and the prediction of customer behaviour, along with the related needs of organizations, it is logical that large computerization companies also want to supply business intelligence (analysis software). This will result in more accurate predictions about the market and developments among individual customers, resulting in an organization being able to respond better to changes in (individual) buying behaviour. This is referred to in this context as agility, whereby an organization has to take advantage of the change in the market.

'This breakthrough search alliance means Yahoo! can focus even more on our own innovative search experience,' said Yahoo! Chief Executive Officer Carol Bartz. 'Yahoo! gets to do what we do best: combine our

science and technology with compelling content to build personally relevant online experiences for our users and customers.'

Microsoft CEO Steve Ballmer concurred with Bartz's assessment. 'Although we are just at the beginning of this process, we have reached an exciting milestone,' Ballmer said. 'I believe that together, Microsoft and Yahoo! will promote more choice, better value and greater innovation to our customers as well as to advertisers and publishers.'

Source: www.finance.yahoo.com.

Being flexible enables the organization to survive in dynamic markets. It is important to know what's going on in the market and to know very quickly. Analysis tools and business intelligence are essential in this respect. Recently (2009) the takeover of SPSS by IBM was announced, which will enable IBM to integrate advanced application of business intelligence into its software portfolio. SAP had previously taken over the company Business Objects with the same intention.

Together, SAP and Business Objects intend to offer high-value solutions for process- and business-oriented professionals. The solutions will be designed to enable companies to strengthen decision processes, increase customer value and create sustainable competitive advantage through real-time, multi-dimensional business intelligence. SAP and Business Objects believe that customers will gain significant business benefits through the combination of new, innovative offerings of enterprise wide business intelligence solutions along with embedded analytics in transactional applications. Additionally, the joint partner ecosystems will be fuelled by the industry's most powerful business process platform providing customers with the best enterprise information management platform available for SAP and non-SAP environments.

Source: mysap.com.

Cross-channel: The Physical Channel and the Internet

A retailer who wishes to be successful both on the Internet and in the physical world has to make clear choices with regards to their strategy. It is best to designate one particular channel as leading and the other channel as supporting.

But it is always important to recognize the customer unambiguously and promptly and to communicate individually with this customer.

For a good shop, the physical channel will lead; the customer will be used to not being recognized or the recognition being at a personal level only (when the salesman recognizes the customer's face). On the Internet, physical recognition is not possible but customer recognition occurs through the input of a login code. The Internet will therefore be primarily supportive of the physical shop. This support can consist of a simple website that only provides a little basic information about the shop or a website where it's possible to place orders (a limited website) but usually only a limited portion of the range is offered.

> *Top multi-channel product category: Consumer electronics purchases have emerged as the most frequently shopped product category among multi-channel shoppers. Apparel, accessories and footwear, home improvement, DIY and appliances came in as the next most popular product categories. In the US, apparel, accessories and footwear, and grocery have the greatest percentage of impulse purchase decisions per basket. In the UK, the grocery market had the highest number of impulse purchase decisions per basket, as well as the largest percentage of impulse shoppers.*

Source: risnews.com, 10 July 2008.

The web-shop is a part of the physical shop but with specific functionalities such as online ordering and home delivery. The Internet can also become a part of the physical shop; the Internet is then used in the shop to support customers in the buying process; to provide specific information or to enable personalization on the basis of customer recognition.

THE SIMPLEST WEBSITE

This website only provides information about the shop such as: general information, location(s), opening hours, probably an e-mail address and other contact information. The aim is to inform the customer in the same way as the telephone book or the Yellow Pages in the past.

A LIMITED WEBSITE

It is possible to offer a limited range, especially for items that require some kind of processing, such as an alteration, a logo on a shirt or printing.

Normally one would have to wait for these articles to be delivered after they have been ordered in-store, but by ordering them online this is perceived as part of the 'delivery time', part of the accepted, standard ordering process. The combination of ordering and collection works well as seen at John Lewis. Customers regard this as an extra service.

Repeat orders of certain articles are also possible. One example of this is Nike. Running shoes have to be specially measured and measured very accurately, but a repeat purchase can be made very easily through the Internet; after all you already know the size, the model and the brand. If you happen to be on the site anyway you could also buy some extra, no-risk articles like a heart rate monitor, food or clothing. Nike has a 'shoefinders' option where you can specify your needs resulting in the suggestion of the correct shoe for you. The shop locator function directs you to your local store which can follow this up by linking their stock to the searched product. E-mail addresses can also be used to notify existing customers of the latest news and special offers.

Taking the physical shop as starting point, adjustments should be based on the buying behaviour of the customers. Consumers seek information on the Internet without a specific site in mind; typing a search word into Google is enough. The information on the retailer's site can therefore be kept restricted to specific buying information and information about the shop. It's logical to let the shop be leading, after all this is a competitive battle with which the retailer is familiar.

On the Internet a completely different battle is being fought; often on rationale, price and trust. Internet suppliers really have to be a member of the home shopping organization and carry the homes shopping warranty logo. This is a mark of trust for customers, the vast majority of whom (80 per cent of buyers) indicate a preference for shopping with an Internet supplier that guarantees speedy delivery, various methods of payment and a money back guarantee. So if the retailer has a shop and fulfils the order via the Internet it would not be logical to apply two different sets of delivery terms and conditions as this would only lead to confusion for the customers.

> Retail research house Verdict values the UK women's underwear market at £3.4bn a year. Lead analyst Maureen Hinton said flagship stores backed by an etail site made sense because of higher business costs compared with the US, but if a site was only transactional in euros it could put off British shoppers.

Source: Retailweek.com, 6 November 2009.

AN INTEGRATED WEBSITE

An Internet supplier who also wants to have a shop has to be aware of the limitations of a physical shop. It is often difficult to maintain the same customer relationship via the Internet as in a shop. The advantages of a physical shop are also clear: there is usually a better relationship with suppliers – who are reticent with respect to Internet suppliers and regard them as less of a threat. After all, the supplier is delivering to a physical shop. The customers can see the articles and take them with them.

A good balance between shop and the Internet is therefore essential and this is difficult for the larger shops. A growing share of the turnover is taking place through the shopping 3.0 behaviour via the Internet. Maintaining only physical shops can optimize the physical buying process but that is insufficient for the large chains. They must respond more strongly to the new shopping behaviour. A customer has to be able to find the shop on the Internet and in the high street. However, that also means there has to be a change of focus.

As was discussed earlier, the Internet is strongly oriented to rationale and customer recognition and physical shopping to transactions and experience. Now a synergy has to be found that links these two approaches at customer level. This means that the customer must be recognized on the Internet just as in the shop, and that some kind of experience has to be created such as the customer is used to in the shop: the same sensation and the same look and feel. That has been nicely accomplished by Victoria's Secret.com, for example, on the basis of the Internet site and the shop experience. The experience in the shop is the same as on the Internet: luxury, warmth, exclusivity and a sense of being pampered. This uniformity is important for the emotional customer bond but in fact customer recognition should also be central.

Victoria's Secret

US fashion and beauty giant Limited Brands has outlined plans to open Victoria's Secret stores in strategic markets including the UK as part of an international expansion drive.

The retailer also intends to set up a dedicated European e-tail site for the brand and is seeking a 'best in continent' franchise partner to launch its cosmetics chain Bath & Body Works.

Speaking at a US investor day, Limited Brands International Executive Vice-President, Martin Waters, said the initiatives were likely within the next few years.

The arrival of both chains would send shockwaves through the industry. However, both sectors are very competitive and some international chains, such as Sephora, have failed to get a foothold in the UK. Limited Brands and Next tried to run Bath & Body Works in the UK in the 1990s but the venture was abandoned.

Waters said that the UK is 'the fashion capital of Europe' and would be a target for flagship Victoria's Secret stores. 'We just need the right site,' he added.

Waters also said that a European website with 'euro fulfilment, transactions in euros, next-day delivery and a returns facility' would 'absolutely' work. 'It will be there for us in future,' he said.

Loyalty programmes were used in the 1990s that made it possible to give good customers extra bonuses, in the form of stamps, discounts or special offers. This system should now be further expanded; it's no longer about *frequency* – how often and how much someone buys – but about loyalty and affinity; about knowing the customers on the basis of their profile, buying history and behaviour, no matter what channel the customer uses.

The information process for customers can also be defined in an informal way. Personal contact with friends and family (seen as experts) is important, but so is the information provided by shop assistants, especially in 'trusted' and well-known shops. Item information is gathered from brochures and brand reputation. A new medium is the Internet, where information is found based on the ORCA model (see Figure 5.3).

It is important to be found on the Internet, via the search term, but the information process phase is also important. Does the customer find the site at the beginning or end of the information process? Sometimes it's not actually a good thing to be at the top of the page on Google or Yahoo, but being in the top ten (on the first page) is. This information is the basis for the purchase.

When important purchases are involved the shops are part of the information process. But if the shop only fulfils the information role there

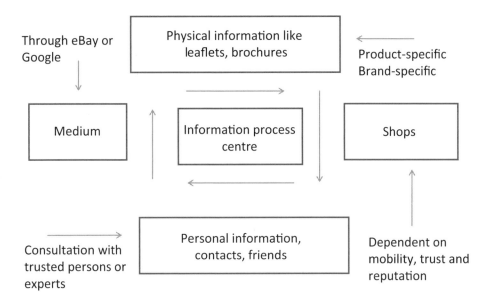

Figure 5.3   Information process for customers

is something wrong with the shop experience. The customer will see the Internet as a preferred channel because of the convenience, service, price or information it offers. The retailer then has to pay more attention to their proposition. The cross-channel functionality is important to large shops. The same computerization system is used both in the shop and on the Internet. There is therefore identical recognition of the individual (login data) and the same product information database. This creates clarity and transparency. Additionally, the platform will also have an e-commerce module for direct communications with customers, an integrated solution in which the customer is central (*customer-centric*). This recognition of customers can be based on a unique login code. The code can be on a card so that the data can be collected and consulted at the checkout or anywhere else in the shop. The possibilities for this are a magnetic card, a chip card, or it may simply be based on name.

Analyzing Customer Behaviour

If the customer had a chip card, like the Oyster card (or Octopus card in Hong Kong), they could hold this to a reader and, together with a sales assistant, analyze their Internet behaviour, justify their choices and decide whether the best choice has been made. This form of support is optimal because it involves both an analysis of customer behaviour and the professional knowledge of the salesman. It's precisely by examining the behaviour together that the customer can be steered towards the right choice. It is much more likely then that the customer will buy in store rather than online.

> *The Octopus card is a rechargeable contactless stored value smart card used to transfer electronic payments in online or offline systems in Hong Kong. Launched in September 1997 to collect fares for the territory's mass transit system, the Octopus card system was the first contactless smart card system in the world and has since grown into a widely used payment system for virtually all public transport in Hong Kong.*
>
> *The Octopus is also used for payment at convenience stores, supermarkets, fast-food restaurants, on-street parking meters, car parks, and other point-of-sale applications such as service stations and vending machines.*

Source: Wikipedia on the Octopus card.

The shop (in combination with a good Internet site) is preferred when buying products that require a high level of advice. A combination of online stores and shops is recommended for the purchase of products requiring less advice. For products requiring little or no advice (convenience goods) it comes down to the customer's personal preference on the basis of convenience and service. A separate approach is then possible.

The calorie-controlled meals from Diako Easyfit are an example of how this distinction can be made. Buying groceries through the Internet is not easy and it is mostly done in the local supermarket unless an advice component is needed. Calorie and protein-controlled meals are an example of this, because the composition is very personal and is often determined in consultation with a dietician. A single intake interview, in person or by telephone is sufficient. After this the profile is built, which enables the customer to place an order through the Internet when additional supplies need to be bought. The customer can also specify any personal preferences regarding flavours, behaviour or supplies when they go on holiday. This means that a grocery product can also be easily sold through the Internet or cross-channel, as Daiko Easyfit is already doing in Germany and the Netherlands.

Cross-channel Computerization[2]

Today's retail challenges require a different approach: a new way of thinking. Today's retail computer-based solutions meet that challenge — and deliver substantial benefits for customer and retailer alike. An innovative retail solution will allow retailers to support customers even better: access to instant information on tailored offers and products, based on historical shopping data. While customers enjoy real-time access to services that provide shopping support, the retailer enjoys the ability to greatly enrich both the CRM database and marketing efforts. The ability to view historical purchases as well as a real-time selection of items in the store enables the extension of relevant offers right at the point of decision (see the ORCA model in Chapter 1) – inside the retail store. As a result, sales promotion and marketing are based on the one-to-one approach just at the buying moment, 'the moment of truth'. The same customer-facing device can be utilized to improve the efficiency and effectiveness of the store employees. They have the information they need to answer customer questions as well as to execute crucial tasks more rapidly, from shelf replenishment to pricing audits, but on top of all this they have information about the customer in front of them!

To make this integration between shop and the Internet easier it is necessary to have an integrated platform. A company which has adopted this philosophy in their product suite is hybris software, a leading player in retail store and Internet integration. Hybris provides a complete multichannel commerce software solution that integrates content, commerce and channel to help retailers (www.hybris.com).

SINGLE SOURCE OF TRUTH FOR PRODUCT DATA – PRODUCT DATA AND SOFTWARE CONSOLIDATION

An integrated system enables a cross-channel approach (Figure 5.4), in which the customer can choose the channel yet is still recognized. This requires a central database system for the shop, the website, customer information, products and commercial communications (brochures, manuals and information). This central system enables unequivocal storage while updates and changes only have to be made once. There is then one customer profile in which their buying and viewing history is recorded. This profile can be accessed via the Internet,

---

2   The application is described on the basis of the hybris system. This system is used by larger retail companies for its cross-channel functionality. The customer and the buying process are the basis of this.

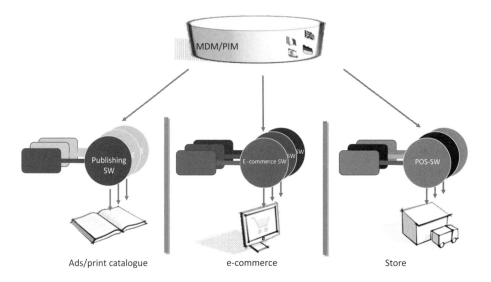

Figure 5.4   Single source of data for product information
Source: Hybris.

offering customers direct support in the search and buying process, but also
in the shop where the customer can search or view information, alone or with
a sales assistant. For that purpose, screens or computer terminals are placed in
the shop which can be activated by the customer (Figure 5.5).

Benefits of an integrated multichannel infrastructure

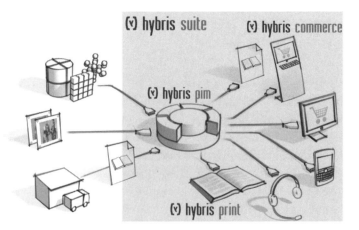

Figure 5.5   Solution overview
Source: Hybris.

SOLUTION OVERVIEW

The hybris system has a number of components enabling this integrated approach, such as a print/catalogue module, a shop and an Internet module. The basis is a central database with product, customer and buying information.

The approach from the perspective of the customers, who decide for themselves whether to buy from a shop or through the Internet, is essential. Specific support will have to be given via the selected medium; this will be different for the Internet and the physical shop.

Table 5.1   Use of the Internet and information technology

Generation	1 seller	2 Sales and service	3 Consistent message	4 Customer-centric
Points of interaction	Stand-alone website	Website Call centre Store	Website Call centre Store Direct mails Direct sale Email	Website Call centre Store Direct mails Direct sale E-mail Chat Click to call Mobile Web
Content and information synchronization	Soloed for web only	Point to point Semi-automated	Synchronized for all points Automated	Synchronized for all points Automated
Business process integration	Soloed for web only	Part of an single process	Single process	Complete customer life cycle
Focus	Soloed treatment for web only	Multichannel	Touchpoint	Process integration

Source: Gartner and Hybris Software.

Development of e-commerce, phase 1, is sales oriented, thereafter service also becomes important. There must be uniform communications and customer recognition when the integration with the shop is implemented. Ultimately, the customer and the buying processes must be the focal point, independent of the channel (Table 5.1). The applications on the Internet depend on the objective, the technological possibilities and the customer's wishes. In the first phase it is based on the transaction orientation that is so typical of the retail sector. Also on the Internet, information about the shop is given and transaction support provided. In the various phases of e-commerce, the first phase is also clearly a selling phase, a well-intended website that is not related to the customers or what happens in the shop; just information about the shop, opening times and location.

In the second phase a separate website is developed and the Internet is regarded as an independent channel. Investments in the Internet increase, the site will be more professional but still focused on the physical shop. Service is important along with selling. The rules of physical purchasing are still regarded as the rules for buying on the Internet. It will be clear that this is not the case. The multichannel strategy (Internet and shop) therefore results in uncertainty amongst customers who don't know what the objective of this is if a separate experience is created on the Internet. The worst shortcoming is the fact that the customer is not central, the product or shop is (transaction orientation). Often too little attention is paid to the customer and the follow-up of e-mails, for example, is very bad. The customer will carry this negative feeling into the physical world. The Internet is then negative for the physical buying behaviour.

Running an Internet strategy 'on the side' is a wrong choice. This soon becomes evident, after which there is usually a harmonization between the shop and the Internet; similar sorts of information and a similar experience. There has to be a separate business plan for the Internet and a separate management accountability. Within the management there has to be agreement on the provision of information, the product range and the prices. This is a synergy model. Finally, the experience must also be transformed into a customer-based strategy, in which the customer and buying processes occupy a central position. This is the most powerful strategy; a strategy that requires integration between channels because the customer is the basis in their buying process (shopping 3.0). The application of the Internet is then noticeable in the shop, in the customer contact and on the Internet. Thus a single source of information is created from which material can be drawn for both the online and offline channels.

Summary

- Shops have to choose where they wish to excel; on the Internet or in the real world.

- Technology should no longer only be focused on making the till transactions and stock management efficient, but must be implemented for the benefit of the customers.

- Shops must have an Internet listing so that customers can find them, at the very least showing contact details and opening times.

- The Internet and the physical shop have to converge, to coalesce with each other. The physical shop is part of an Internet strategy and the Internet has to be brought into the shop as part of the buying and selling process.

- Cross-channel, the integration between the shop and the Internet, is where the future lies. Technology is a precondition for this.

- Customers have to be recognized and steered. Near field communication, location-based services and event-driven communication on the basis of algorithms are useful aids.

- The technology has to be based on the buying process: orientation and information through the Internet, but buying can be done in the shop or on the Internet. This integration demands an integral approach to the technology and an integrated technological platform.

- The real future is in cross-retailing: a physical shop with Internet access for customer and buying support in the store and a web-shop on the Internet. Orders can be collected from the shop. The best of both worlds supported by an integrated software platform like hybris.

Shopping

1. In 2008, 73 per cent of individuals said that their household had ordered goods via the Internet, phone or post for delivery, with 37 per cent receiving deliveries at least monthly. In the 2002 research, the respective figures were 64 per cent and 27 per cent.

2.   The proportion of deliveries ordered via the Internet has increased, from 26 per cent in the 2002 research to 73 per cent in the 2008 research.

3.   Although there has been an increase in the ordering of food and drink for home delivery over the period, home deliveries only account for a small proportion of food shopping. In 2008, 4 per cent of those responsible for the main household food shop said they usually had the main food shop delivered.

For almost a fifth (17 per cent) of home deliveries someone in the household visited an outlet prior to purchasing the item (15 per cent), made the trip to collect an item left at the post office/depot/outlet (3 per cent) or made a trip to return the item (<1 per cent).

Source: www.dft.gov.uk.

Case Study: Blue Tomato

Blue Tomato is a leading Austria-based retailer of sportswear and sports equipment, specializing in winter sports, and has shops in major towns like Wien and Graz. Just before the winter season in 2009, Blue Tomato opened a new web portal, featuring an online magazine, newsletter and multimedia content. The company started life as a classical retailer but has had an online prescence since 1997. The launch of the new portal demonstrates a commitment to integrate the Internet as part of the total retail concept.

The success of the present website www.bluetomato.at is based on its intuitive navigation and improved product presentation. The more intense and personalized communication will lead to increased traffic and sales (up 30 per cent in the last year).

SOLUTION

A centralized and media-neutral product information management system (hybris), is connected via an interface with an inventory control system so orders can be processed very quickly. For communication, the half-yearly catalogue can be printed directly using various layout programmes. This way more frequent publications are made possible which will lead directly to more traffic and sales. By combining the strong customer base of the shops with the online potential, customer contact is more intense and the communication more direct.

Case Study: Waterstone's

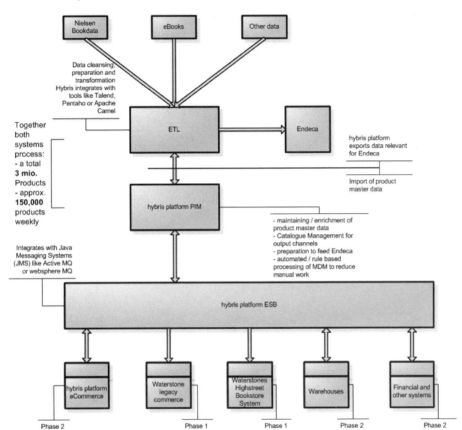

Figure 5.6   The software solution

Waterstone's introduced its website in 2006 and since then growth has been rapid. The website offers a catalogue of over three million books, including the fast-growing new format of e-book downloads. The selection of hybris Commerce followed detailed analysis of the challenges currently faced by Waterstone's and of its ambitious growth plans.

David Kohn, Head of E-Commerce at Waterstone's, said:

> *Our online business is currently growing rapidly and we have demanding targets and expectations for our future growth in this channel. In order to compete effectively online, we need an e-Commerce solution that delivers all of the basics effectively, but which is also flexible and allows for our*

future development. We also require a top-class PIM system to handle our large and growing catalogue to sit at the heart of our multi channel retail strategy. Hybris will allow us to address all of our needs in one platform.

Phase 1 of this project was to implement hybris PIM to predominantly feed both the existing e-commerce platform (IBM Websphere) and the Endeca search and navigation solution. This went live in September 2009 and work has now commenced in replacing the commerce element with hybris Commerce which will greatly facilitate and accelerate the catalogue synchronization process.

It is still very early to recognize specific returns on investment (ROIs) except that it has already reduced the time of importing and validating the full Nielson feed from two days to a few hours.

The architecture diagram can be seen on the previous page (Figure 5.6) for Phase 1 (live) and Phase 2:

Case Study: Scholl

QUICK FACTS

Geographical scope: Global roll-out

Solution overview: Global e-commerce platform for B2C

Technology: hybris Commerce, hybris Customer Management System (CMS)

Integration: Tight integration to global SAP implementation

Reference person: Waseem Haq, Head of Web and E-commerce Solutions, introduction provided on request

Budget: Confidential, only provided by customer directly

OVERVIEW

Scholl, the global footwear and footcare brand, is part of the SSL International portfolio of brands, which also includes Durex and a range of locally owned over the counter (OTC) products such as Full Marks, Medised and Paramol in the UK. Scholl brands range from its Party Feet gel insole range to Flight Socks and the iconic Scholl Pescura sandal, which is 50 years old this year. SSL has a turnover of more than £500m with £68m operating profit. SSL has operations in 35 countries across Europe, Asia Pacific and the Americas, which sell into over 100 countries worldwide and also has manufacturing operations in India, Thailand, China and the UK. SSL employs around 5,000 people globally.

CHALLENGE

Scholl had outgrown its previous e-commerce system which was not capable of supporting the 'problem–solution journey' that SSL International's direct sales channel needs to provide to today's online consumer.

It needed to find an e-commerce platform that would support the functionality and flexibility required to provide the online shopping experience that consumers now expect, with the robustness and scalability necessary to cope with increased volumes of web traffic and corresponding business growth as SSL International replaces existing brand sites in other territories.

They want to significantly improve their online channel and are looking to drive revenue through web stores.

- Feature-rich B2C multi-site solution

- Sophisticated call centre solution

- Tight integration with SAP for stock management and multi-distribution centre fulfilment

- Tight integration with Sharepoint via web services for content management (Durex platform only)

SOLUTION

SSL purchased a global licence of hybris Commerce and used Javelin Group's modular 'hybris plus' solution called Camel Commerce to address SSL International's long-term goals. Camel Commerce combines the multichannel, multi-language and multi-currency capabilities for which hybris is best known with additional best practice e-commerce functionality and integration with market-leading applications for order management, search and navigation, personalization, analytics and customer ratings. The opportunity to cross-sell and up-sell is supported by sophisticated promotional and merchandizing capabilities and an efficient checkout process, maximizing average order value (AOV).

BENEFITS

The launch of the revised UK e-commerce website for Scholl has led to a significant increase in online sales and web traffic for www.scholl.com. It also marks the first phase in SSL International's long-term commitment to providing direct consumer interaction with the brand. SSL International, which is represented in over 100 countries throughout the world, now plans to roll out the website to overseas markets, starting in Europe from July, followed by the consideration of emerging market requirements.

6

The Future of Shopping: Shopping, the Internet or Both?

The future of shopping is actually a combination of technology and experience, of Internet and store-based shops. This defines the behaviour of the buyers. The Internet is still only at the beginning of its development, the shopping centres have not, by a long chalk, adjusted to the demands of shopping 3.0 and consumers are still searching for the most desirable form. The Internet offers everything, but does that make it the shopping centre of the future? A lot will depend on the technological developments, but societal, social and economic developments will also be definitive for the future of shopping. In the end it is still the customer who defines what the future will look like. Customers still have the same wishes as they had decades ago, only the possibilities have changed.

The Décor Changes, Not the Customer

Perhaps the change had already started with the Industrial Revolution in the nineteenth century. City centres were developed, mass production began and there was more affluence and leisure, however modest that was. Shopping as a leisure activity, especially for luxury items, came into vogue. In the twentieth century shopping became increasingly professional, shopping centres emerged, shops became more attractive and advertising developed. Customers were increasingly attracted by these fine shops and enticed by the promises made in the advertising. This laid the basis for the current status of shopping.

Until the start of this century, shopping had been synonymous with 'going to the shops'. The mail order sector had only a modest share of consumer spending; those who ordered from mail order companies were mainly the lower social classes living out in the countryside. Mail order companies offered an attractive catalogue with an extensive range. Often these items were not on sale locally, ideal for buyers from rural areas. It was also possible to pay in instalments, no questions asked, so that the less well-off could buy attractive items too. This was, of course, a first indication of what the future would bring; after all, these companies met the needs of their customers, without regard to location. This has become an important condition for survival for mail order companies. These companies were members of the mail order association, which was later incorporated into the home shopping organization, of which traditional mail order is still a part.

The growth of department stores and out-of-town shopping centres meant that, gradually, more and more small retailers, often family-run shops, had to abandon the streets to the large retail chains.

LOSS OF LOCAL TRADERS

Up to the end of the 1950s the Dutch shopping street looked very different to now.

It was the era of traditional local traders. Shops were run by small independent businessmen, as the boss in their own shop, who kept the business going together with his wife and children. The family lived behind or above the shop. Everything centred around the customer, hard work and never any spare time.

After the Second World War the local traders encountered increasing difficulties. With the opening of the first self-service grocers at the end of the 1940s came the rise of supermarkets in the Netherlands.

While in other sectors the small shops were also unable to compete against the large-scale shopping concerns. Within twenty years 100,000 independent shops disappeared from the streets. They were replaced by branches of large retail chains, with the result that many shopping streets in the Netherlands now look almost identical.

Source: verreverwanten/vv.netrex.nl.

In the 1960s more and more shopping centres appeared: small-scale neighbourhood shopping centres as well as large centres. These centres served as a sort of magnet to attract customers. A supermarket, a pharmacy, a clothing shop and some sort of general household shop were usual. In fact these were centres for the daily shopping, for convenience goods. The luxurious centres and the so-called 'shopping goods' stores concentrated in centres where shopping was in fact intended to be fun: city centres and, later, luxurious shopping centres. This development was further enhanced by increasing mobility. Cars had become common and shopping by car became the norm. Shopping centres that were further out of town therefore became accessible to a larger group of people, and the car also made it possible to buy in larger quantities. The daily shopping, which used to be bought from local traders, became weekly grocery shopping at supermarkets with car parks. This was at the expense of the local traders who were not located close together (they were positioned on long main streets or between houses). This resulted in shops locating closer to each other, making shopping locally more efficient and more fun.

The bankruptcy of Woolworths led to a lot of shops suddenly becoming available in the so-called A1 locations, on high streets and in shopping centres. Customers associated these locations with the low-price image of Woolworths. It was interesting to see what would happen with these locations, given the new buying behaviour (Internet and supermarkets as new low-price retailers) and the decrease in turnover of the shops due to the recession. During a period of eight months (between 1 January 2009 and 31 August 2009) 60 per cent were re-leased (a total of 480 shops). Of these, 37 per cent (134) were leased to other low-price shops that elaborated on the image of the location and the association with the neighbourhood (buyer's public), 31 per cent (110) were taken up by supermarkets and the remaining 32 per cent became clothing shops for chains like New Look and Peacocks. The explanation for this was that buyers expected a low-price shop in the Woolworths' location, but also that supermarkets were looking to expand their market share, especially in this sector. They could realize this market expansion primarily in new locations. For clothing shops, it was in fact the location that was important; lots of people, top location and large premises. This enabled them to display a large collection. It is especially by displaying this large collection that they offer an alternative to Internet shopping.

> The void on the UK's high streets left by the collapse of Woolworths has been predominantly filled by pound stores and discount retailers, in a stark indication of how the credit crisis has reshaped the retail industry.

> The market conditions have been instrumental in dictating the type of retailers that have acquired the ex-Woolworths sites. 'Research

indicates that fashion operators moved to acquire large, prime units, in the strongest trading locations, enabling them to display a full range of stock, whereas the discounters and grocers have looked to take advantage of the current market and gain market share where they can.'

Source: *Daily Telegraph*, 27 August 2009.

The three-way split in buying behaviour (convenience, shopping and luxury) which arose in recent decades on the basis of shop location, is also the basis for the shopping 3.0 behaviour of customers. Everyone still wants to be able to buy convenience goods locally and efficiently; either all in one shop or in shops that are close to each other. Local shops will always remain important for that, but through the transparency in the market and the increasing pressure on prices they will no longer be small independent shops only. There will also be large well-known retail chains in these local centres, as a sort of magnet. The local shops will not compete with these shops but offer a supplementary range. The strength of the local range and the embedding in the local community will lead to a mixture of well-known shops and local shops. The strengths of these well-known shops include the very fact that they are widely known, their special offers and the universal range of products. The local shops' strength is their local embedding, and the fact that the range is often geared to the local needs and service. More and more large retail chains are recognizing this and choosing to open smaller shops with a focused range. This capitalizes on shopping 3.0 in which being small scale and offering good service is increasingly important for physical shops. The main retail chains are opening smaller shops in neighbourhood shopping centres or villages (this may or may not be in a franchise formula).

People will also shop, in peace and quiet, for luxury items, especially self-indulgence products. An afternoon out is then perfectly normal. You don't mind travelling into town or to a large shopping centre where there's plenty choice and amusement on offer. Even a day trip to another city or across the border is a possibility. London, Manchester, Antwerp and Düsseldorf are well known as shopping cities, and people quite often spend a shopping weekend in London, staying in a good hotel and seeing a show in the West End. Shopping for luxury items is part of spoiling oneself, of recreational shopping. Shopping as an activity is then much more important than the item purchased. The shop (service and luxury), the surroundings, and the personal feeling also play an important role in this. After all, a Rolex isn't handed to the customer in a brown paper bag!

SHOPPING IN THE NINETEENTH CENTURY

Shopping as a leisure activity is actually a fairly new phenomenon. It was only in 1880 that the word shopping was first used. Prior to that, products were delivered to the home by regular suppliers, for example, or peddlers. The day-to-day shopping was done by maids at the market or in the meat markets, and so-called decent women were expected to stay indoors.

One of the causes of the rise of shopping as such was the advent of mass production in factories. This meant that products became cheaper, so that more people could buy things. In the 19th century it also became possible to produce large shop windows, so that shop goods would be attractively displayed in the windows. It became fashionable for well-to-do women to stroll past the beautiful shop windows. In main cities for instance the shops were open until 10pm, even on Sundays! Like nowadays the shops in high streets sold luxury goods such as clothing, home accessories and all sorts of knick-knacks.

John Lewis Newcastle (formerly Bainbridge) in Newcastle upon Tyne is the world's oldest department store. It is still known to many of its customers as Bainbridge, despite the name change to 'John Lewis'. The Newcastle institution dates back to 1838 when Emerson Muschamp Bainbridge, aged 21, went into partnership with William Alder Dunn and opened a draper's and fashion shop in Market Street, Newcastle.

In terms of retailing history, one of the most significant facts about the Newcastle Bainbridge shop, is that as early as 1849 weekly takings were recorded by department, making it the earliest of all department stores. This ledger survives and is kept in the John Lewis archives. John Lewis bought the Bainbridge store in 1952.

John Lewis Newcastle retained its original name of Bainbridge until 2002, when the store was rebranded as John Lewis Newcastle.

Source: Wikipedia in John Lewis Department stores.

The role of technology varies across all three groups, based on buying behaviour (Table 6.1). With convenience goods, the technology will be used to make the grocery shopping more efficient, with shopping goods it will be used to encourage the purchase of items and to promote the purchase of more articles (such as already occurs with the recommended articles on Amazon. com, for example). In a shop, purchase suggestions will also be given this way.

Table 6.1   Buying preferences based on types of articles

	Convenience goods	Shopping goods	Luxury items
Shop benefits	Convenience shop. Close to home. Routine purchases.	No specific preference. Dependent on personal circumstances (time, preference, location). Conscious choices.	Specific personal preference. Large indulgence effect. Conviviality and service are important. High perception content.
Internet benefits	Strong physical role of shopping. Internet for special items (such as wine and dietary articles). Important role of RFID for articles and customers.	Strong virtual role in shopping. Physical also supported with virtual applications. Internet plays an important role. Becoming increasingly emotion oriented. Cross-channel applications based on Internet (and RFID).	Strong physical role in shopping, supported with virtual applications. Internet for information and experience.

With luxury articles the technology will in fact contribute to the creation of the luxurious ambience and a good mood. The barriers to buy will be lowered and the happy feeling that comes with the purchase enhanced. Through their experience with the Internet, customers will also become familiar with the specific features of the online store. Customers are recognized, the purchase amount is recorded and suggestions for other articles are given. These suggestions are based on historic buying behaviour, profile matching and the articles viewed. Customers experience this as support in the buying process. The system records everything and makes customers feel they are being helped. Profile matching is especially important because suggestions are made on the basis of buying profiles. Therefore, if a person buys something this could also be a suggestion for a different person with the same buying characteristics. The behaviour is then important. This form of buying support is behaviour driven (behavioural targeting). It's important that the suggestions match the wishes of the customer, as this generates confidence, but it is also habit forming.

Googling Becomes Buying on the Basis of Preferences and Suggestions

On the basis of my music purchases, for example, suggestions can be made for other music purchases, but suppose the music purchases I make could also provide suggestions for the purchase of books, holidays or clothing. The basis of these recommendations is made by profile matching. Customers can also make use of this facility proactively. For example, if you have read a good book and you would like hear suggestions for another book that matches the atmosphere and type of book that you have enjoyed, then it is possible to search proactively on the basis of this. This sort of buying behaviour support leads to habit forming. Customers also want this in a shop and place specific demands on the sales staff; they have to be familiar with the customer's preferences and with the possible article associations. However, customers will also research the items they want to buy on the Internet before visiting the physical shop to make the purchase. Use of the Internet is not restricted to searching for specific items; it is also used to find suggestions for associated articles.

This is a big change from the normal style of shopping and resembles 'googling'. This focused search by the customer, on the basis of suggestions made on the Internet, will become the basis of shopping in the future. This will also happen in the shop with a cross-channel platform or event-oriented software. Shops have to be prepared for very articulate and explicit customers. The sales technique used in the shop can also help with such things as narrowcasting, suggestions, Internet pillars and Near Field Communication, as will be discussed later. The message is that customers get used to the behaviour and service of the Internet and expect it for physical shopping. They allow themselves to be led more and more by suggestions instead of looking themselves. Knowledge of customers, customer behaviour and product preferences and associations are becoming increasingly important in the act of shopping. The application of technology is consequently indispensable.

New Business Models Needed

The changes that arise from the combination of technology and shopping 3.0 also enables new business models. Using a cost price-plus model based on individual transactions will no longer suffice. New ways of making money have to be found, for example by means of a fixed subscription rate, by asking suppliers to pay for space on the shelves or through advertisers paying for contact with customers. The success of the retail trade in the future will in fact be determined by the creativity shown in devising new business models. Examples of this include Google (charges for an entry with search terms), eBay (charges for specific entries and search terms, sometimes also for special advertisements) and virus scanners that charge for updates. This creativity is also important in the new (virtual) products, as Apple has demonstrated with iTunes (pay per number) and should now be demonstrated with e-books.

E-BOOK SALES PREDICTIONS TOO OPTIMISTIC

Forecasts that the UK's e-book market will grow to £710m by 2013 are 'way off', said a senior figure at Nielsen Book, claiming sales would not climb that high for 'quite some time'.

Speaking at yesterday's (13th October) Tools of Change conference at the Frankfurt Book Fair, Ann Betts, Commercial Director for Nielsen Book, highlighted three estimates for e-book sales by 2013. The 'high case' estimate was for sales reaching half of the viable e-book market – or number of titles that are available to be formatted into e-books – which is expected to be just over £1.4bn.

Betts acknowledged the rapid growth seen in the digital market in recent years, particularly in the US, citing Citigroup's estimate that 550,000 Kindles had been sold by the end of last year in America, and 'various' estimates that put that at 1m this summer. However, Betts said: 'I don't see the UK market going there.' She said the 'high case' estimate would be 'quite a challenge' given the nature of the current print book market, which would require at least 25% of all books to be converted into e-books. In order for the market to grow to that size, she argued that 12m devices would have to be sold. 'That's about one-fifth of the UK population, and this is all of the book-buying public,' Betts said. Betts suggested a number of households would be likely to share devices, as they share books. She added the current economic climate would slow the rate of growth 'in the short term'. She also referred to a recent study, showing that 35% of UK consumers wanted devices to be priced below £100, but the most persuasive factor was the price of e-books, which was the main concern of almost half (46%) of respondents. 'Consumers are exceptionally price sensitive at the moment, and will be for at least two years,' she said.

Source: www.thebookseller.com, 14 October 2009.

Examples of the Application of Virtual Technology in Shops

CONVENIENCE GOODS

On the shopping trolley there is a small screen which displays a shopping list. This list can be automatically loaded from the customer's USB stick and can also be loaded online through an Internet link with devices in the home. Articles can be scanned using an RFID chip. This chip (the size of a grain of sand) is added to the article by the manufacturer. All the information about the food item, such as production date, shelf life, ingredients, allergy information and retail price are stored on the chip. The article can be scanned contactlessly (via a laser beam in the reader). The customer can therefore determine whether the article might invoke an allergic reaction, what is in it, what the use by/sell by date is and whether they can also get menu suggestions. Offering menu suggestions could entail listing ingredients that belong to a certain recipe. These could then become recommended purchases shown on a list on a screen on the shopping trolley, similarly to how articles are recommended on the Internet but actually on the shop floor. The retailer can use the chip for faster payment at the checkout and for theft prevention.

By placing readers in kitchen cupboards and in the refrigerator there can be constant monitoring of whether there are sufficient supplies at home. When entering the shop a personal code is assigned to the trolley, after which the home stock situation is loaded and an electronic shopping list created. The customer can of course decide whether or not to buy these groceries or deviate from the list. The traditional style of grocery shopping with a list acquires a new dimension this way. The shop can add to this list with special offers and also with associated products, as we've just seen with the menu suggestions.

It goes without saying that the purchases are automatically registered for personalized offers (for example, discounts or savings stamps). At home the articles are placed in the cupboards and the reader will register this too. All the actions are contactless so that customers no longer have to think about these purchases. One such emerging technology could be augmented reality – an interactive way to simulate imagery and graphics onto a physical environment.

Last year, Tobi applied augmented reality to its 'Fashionista' virtual dressing room, where customers can use a Web cam image of their bodies to try on garments to check style and fit. What makes the Fashionista unique is that it captures real-time images with personalized products using live Web footage of a customer rather than relying on a static photo or generic avatar. While it remains to be seen how technology such as the 'Fashionista' virtual dressing can be monetized, Tobi experimented with augmented reality because the company wants to be a leader in innovating the online fashion user experience.

Sukhinder Singh Cassidy, chief executive officer of fashion social-networking site Polyvore, predicts that companies will continue to work on the elements that are missing from shopping online.

'I think for the future of fashion online, it is about bringing the thrill of discovery and serendipity into e-tail shopping, as well as leveraging real-time data (e.g., top trends, products, sites, brands) into insights for consumers and brands,' Singh Cassidy said.

Source: www.apparelnews.net, 13 May 2010.

For those who want to shop even more efficiently it is sufficient to enter a minimum stock into the system. The retailer can then fulfil an order accordingly and deliver the groceries to the home. It will also be possible to do a stock scan in the evening and to tick a list created on the basis of the recommended shopping list and send it to the supermarket, choosing between home delivery and collection. This use is based on an RFID chip like those used now in, for example, the OV chip card (a Dutch public transport card), a small screen on the shopping trolley, a reader at home in the storage cupboards and the Internet.

All these techniques are already available. Linking them is therefore simply a question of time (as regards facilities) and a sense of demand and necessity from customers. The features are recognition of the product (the chip), a contactless reader and a link to a central database to enable support independent of location. In the case of convenience goods this will lead to cost savings and efficiency when buying. The patterns are then comparable with the applications on the Internet. The customer only has to complete the physical transaction themself and take the articles home or choose to have the retailer deliver them.

SHOPPING GOODS

The same technique is possible here. By fitting a chip to an article, associated items can be recommended. Standing in front of a fitting room mirror with an item of clothing, other items can be recommended: a jacket to go with a pair of trousers, a scarf, a shirt or a tie. One way of doing this is to show them in the mirror when you stand in front of it. The chip in the item of clothing then forms the basis for the suggestions. However, this can also be made personal. A chip in the customer card or phone, with personal details, could also be the basis for suggestions. It's then possible to refer to a particular size or a previous purchase. A link can also be made with a particular Internet site for extra information about the article or the purchase thereof. The light can also be adjusted in the same way. When trying on an evening dress dimmed light could be used in the fitting room and bright light for a summer dress. The chip would adjust the ambient lighting to make this as realistic as possible, depending on the atmosphere desired. This would make buying more personal and more pleasant.

The Internet could also be integrated into the shop as well. By installing screens or pillars the customer can consult the Internet before buying. The shop then has the great advantage of personal contact and actually having the articles in the shop. The sales assistant and customer can also look at the Internet together during the buying process. The sales assistant can make suggestions and point out differences. In this way the sales conversation becomes supportive of the buying process. Buying in-store then becomes more logical. It is also possible to spontaneously project messages onto screens. At present these are often product-based messages for a mass audience, everyone can see them. But if there was a smaller screen and perhaps individual recognition, personal messages would also be possible. The example of the fitting room is illustrative of this point. More information is provided and other articles are recommended in the fitting room on the basis of the article. If there is also personal recognition then a suggestion could be made on the basis of historic buying behaviour or profile matching, for example. What is then possible on the Internet is also possible in the fitting room. In effect there is a convergence of technology and application. Narrowcasting then becomes very personal and no longer sale oriented, but rather purchase supporting.

The application of near field communication is comparable. Addressing customers personally in a certain environment can generate extra affinity. Simple examples are communication oriented. If you are walking in the high street you can receive personal messages from the shops in the street. This could result in customers being drawn to the shop. The disadvantage of this approach is that it is very obtrusive and often leads to irritation. The mobile phone is the medium that betrays your location and is immediately also the medium used for the communication that occurs. If the telephone also has an RFID chip with relevant personal details, such as age, gender or buying intentions, the messages can be very personalized. This draws visitors to the shop. In fact, this would seem to be a future development of the Internet, in which users will increasingly be approached proactively, as soon as they become visible online.

LUXURY ITEMS

The purchase of luxury items is often a physical experience: setting off, going to the shop, seeing, looking, feeling and buying. Shopping for luxury items is a pleasure – you choose a particular shopping street or a particular shop, you have gathered a lot of information and looked at alternatives in advance. It's time to spoil yourself! The anticipation starts at home, of course, and the Internet plays a significant role in this. You search for shops selling the item you are looking for and examine the product on the Internet, perhaps even viewing videos or weblogs. Your sense of excitement grows, especially from discussing it with others. The purchase is made and, then, with a spring in your step you head for home to show it off to anyone who has a few moments! That feeling of excitement is difficult to match online, where the buying process remains clinical, despite the beautiful sites with colours and videos.

In a shop the pleasure of buying can be intensified by the interior, the colours, the atmosphere, the friendly staff and even being offered something to drink. Technology can also be useful too: by adjusting the lighting to suit the product (as in the fitting room), or in the shop; by displaying extra information on the mirror, such as who else has bought the product (celebrities, for example), information about related items and the product itself, or possible colour combinations. The moment of purchase has to be pleasant and give the customer a warm feeling. This can be done very easily by adjusting the lighting to the time of day, to the product or to the customer, or by using the mirror as a screen to display extra information, and finally by registration and use of as much customer data as possible. If the customer can be expected to return frequently, then a loyalty card, with RFID chip, can be provided which is automatically read when the customer next visits so that they are recognized.

All of this results in a very personal approach that increases the customer's affinity with the shop and makes the customer feel even more at home. The role of the Internet is a supportive one in terms of the purchase of luxury items, but it can play a role in later communications and for any interaction in the future.

Thus new products can be offered or services proposed so that the customer will come back to the shop; like cleaning your diamond ring or polishing your gold jewellery. This can be done by communicating directly through the shop's site on the basis of historic buying behaviour and customer recognition. E-mail is used for active customer approaches and the site can be used for passive communications if customers are logged in (communication via IP address is also possible).

Changes in the Online Buying Process

Buying via the Internet will also change, because technology makes more possible and because customers acquire more and more experience in using the Internet as a shopping medium. The convenience of the Internet channel is precisely what is important. An article can be found very quickly, the right information obtained and the order can be placed. At present this is carried out by the buyer; who has to go looking for products and information. The supplier, the shop, has to be found. But this will change as a result of the Internet being categorized differently. Right now it's still one big mess of suppliers in which the user has to find their way. It's conceivable that this will not be the case in the future. The simplest way will then be customer recognition. Buyers will be directed immediately to the correct offer. Just by logging in, suggestions will appear on the screen. The customer feels at home with the offer and doesn't need to search any longer for the desired products. There will be two routes on a site: the suggested purchases on the basis of customer and behaviour recognition, and a route for the customer who searches independently. This results in a stronger connection with customers who will benefit from buying time and again from the same site. Suppliers therefore obtain more and more knowledge about the customers' behaviour and better suggestions can be made. Why should the customer do it the hard way?

This technique is based on a personal login screen in which the links are activated by the user or by recently visited sites. Actions currently performed by the user – marking pages (bookmarks), saving sites or files on your desktop – will no longer be necessary. As soon as you log in all relevant sites will automatically be activated and accessible to the visitor. A screen with icons or a search menu will be visible. These sites receive a signal that you are online and activate a communication module; this can result in a message appearing immediately on the user's screen. At present there are no general applications of this that can activate multiple sites. However, Skype users can set up the program so that they are immediately visible online as soon as their computer is started and they can send each other messages directly that are visible on the screen. Facebook users can also see how many friends are online and which friends they are. Chatting is then made very simple indeed.

This application provides a basis for a personal web page with intelligent links and the user need no longer start looking for their favourite page or supplier straight away. Naturally, this is only possible for a limited number of sites but again there is a restriction in the buying behaviour. Customers make 80 per cent of their purchases at less than five shops and 80 per cent of Internet use occurs on fewer than five sites. It all seems so unrestricted, both the choice in the shop and the choice on the Internet, but the behaviour of buyers is inhibited. People want to keep the overview; they have their preferences and routines. Routine gives them something to go on and provides security; they don't like deviating from a pattern. The customer gets used to his home town, shops, the layout in the shops and the products stocked. This connection is important because it creates a threshold for similar suppliers and products. This same behaviour is seen on the Internet and technology will increasingly facilitate behaviour automatically – as in the example of the personalized home page (Figure 6.1).

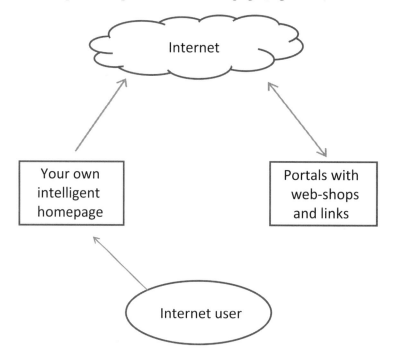

Figure 6.1   Intelligent home portals

Users of the Internet could have their own intelligent home page in which the most frequently visited sites are already pre-programmed. This is a direct interaction and communication based on prepared communications and is a choice of the user. Suppliers will also collaborate in portals on the basis of products, matching customer profiles or location.

However, before a particular site can be found, a change will have occurred. Suppliers will need to collaborate to a greater extent and move 'closer' to each other. The trend that occurred in the physical world in the 1960s will also occur on the Internet. Customers will not want to keep searching and surfing to locate a supplier. The continued use of Google to find sites demonstrates this, however, only occasionally does anyone look further than the first page of results. Purchases are more likely to be made on top-of-mind sites, known names or sites that have been bookmarked. A logical categorization will mean there is no need for extensive searching. This categorization could arise through the offer being combined on the basis of shopping centres or forces being joined on the basis of products, buyer's profiles or associations.

> In the 19ᵗʰ century the first department stores appeared, which broke with the traditional retail sector. They adopted a new formula: everything-under-one-roof (all products can be bought in the same shop), self-service, fixed, low sales prices and immediate payment instead of buying on credit. One of the very first department stores in the world was 'Au Bon Marché', which opened in Paris in 1872.

Source: www.twintigeeuwennederland.nl.

Physical shops can team up to form an online shopping centre. Customers can then either buy in the physical shopping centre or on the Internet. Internet retailers may also be offered the opportunity of a place in the online shopping centre. Various product portals can offer access to suppliers, such as wine portals, holiday portals or clothing portals. There is no need to keep searching for suppliers – the portals provide the access to the Internet – and buyers will return sooner because products are easily located. A customer relationship can be built up on the basis of the portal, so that the individual retailers don't have to carry out this activity themselves. This efficiency is primarily in the interest of customers who will suffer from a surfeit of e-mails and newsletters. The buying suggestion can then be done at portal level.

Combining forces on the basis of buyers' profiles often consists of combining on the basis of demographic characteristics. A ladies' site, a men's site, a sports site, a seniors' web, teenagers' web, but also social sites all attract a certain profile; they are attractive to a particular group, as is the case with Facebook and Linkedin. Special offers must then target that group precisely. Associations are sites that have a defined core; on the basis of this target group they can attract associated product suppliers. This could be a booking site, like those used by airlines or hotels, to which hotels, holiday retailers and taxi companies can be connected. The search engines of Yahoo and Microsoft (Bing) have this application. This is an indication of the future of the Internet in the buying process for customers. Information is separated from the buying process.

A number of suggestions are made for more specific searches on the basis of the first search term. When searching for a car make, for example, it's possible to search for accessories or videos of this specific make. The user can then make the search more specific, for example according to the colour of the car. Within the search environment Bing also offers a number of additional functionalities. Thus the Internet user can choose the desired price category for restaurants, flights or hotels. An overview of relevant evaluations by users, derived from popular comparison sites, is also possible. Bing consequently competes directly with comparison sites.

The search machine takes the location of the user, if relevant, into account in calculating search results. Because of the region-specific functions, Microsoft is launching the search machine by country.

Until now the Internet was, in effect, one big mess of websites. They were often not linked (despite the possibilities of hyperlinks) and there was little collaboration. Internet users had to find their own way around and this offered Google the chance to open up the Internet and to become the most important online player. The result was that Internet users started using Google en masse to find information and sites. If Google couldn't find it then it didn't exist in the eyes of users; they were impatient and seldom satisfied, so most of them never got much further than the first ten entries. As a result of increasing experience, and because competitors are looking for ways to challenge Google, use of the Internet is entering a new phase. This started in 2008 and, based on the developments described in Chapter 3, it can be called the Internet phase. In this phase, the Internet will develop in its own way and the behaviour of users will be based, amongst other things, on the opportunities it offers. The behaviour in the pre-Internet phase was, in effect, a continuation of the existing behaviour,

facilitated by a new medium. This is actually normal when new possibilities
and technologies arise. The first car was a horse and cart, without the horse
but with an engine; the first accounting programmes had a ledger and journal
entries; and the first Internet sites had advertisements in the form of a banner
– what else is new? The behaviour of Internet users shows that there really
is structure in the use of the Internet, both on the basis of the buying process
and on the basis of preferences – personal and in groups. This behaviour is
the foundation of Internet anthropology in which the behaviour of users is
researched. This behaviour is in some respects perhaps similar to the behaviour
displayed in the physical world, but different in other respects. Returning to
the basis of 'being human' the behaviour resembles that of the prehistoric
tribes: people seek each other out, live in congenial groups or groups that have
a particular common goal, and they communicate. Benschop concluded that it
resembles the traditional tribes but then without the physical boundaries:

> The self-organising virtual communities have much in common with
> traditional tribes. The virtual tribe communities form a new type of
> social reality. It is a social reality that is not delimited by physical
> boundaries. It has no territory that has to be controlled and defended by
> the legitimate force and laws of a single state. And it also has no specific
> government or alliance of governments that can regulate these new
> social relationships, networks and communities. Tim North describes
> this tribal society as follows: 'Given the fact that the technological
> societies in the world all are characterised by a state structure [Service
> 1971] and that the Net society embodies a high level of technology, it
> is a matter of some surprise to find that its political organisation has
> more in common with that of simple hunter-gatherer societies than it
> does with the state. It may be that all this technology has enabled us to
> come "full circle", in a sense. The simple egalitarianism of band-tribal
> structures may be a more natural condition for us than our impersonal
> cities and nation-states. There is a certain elegance to the notion that
> the Net, one of the crowning achievements of our techno-industrial
> Western societies, may be instrumental in enabling us to return to a
> simpler, more egalitarian and more socially interactive way of life.'

Source: Dr. Albert Benschop, UvA.[1]

More order is appearing on the Internet, boundaries are being defined
for its use and the user is dealing with the new medium in a more informed

---

1   www.sociosite.net.

manner. The split in information and buying behaviour is a consequence of this. To find material on the Internet, one has to search through the vast amounts of information available, and Google provides an effective medium for this. The requirement for information is often defined by the moment and the need is also often not recurring – once you know something there's no need to go looking for it again. It's different with buying. Within a buying process there is a need for information, for experiences, for knowledge about web-shops and perhaps for a whole lot more. This need is less unambiguous but is linked to other needs: via orientation to information about shops for instance. There are associative needs based on the search question; a need that Google does not meet. The functionality of Google is based on the conventional approach to searching, but now the Internet is able to offer more. Suppliers are joining forces as described above, users are even making links on their own personal home page, but the function of searching will also change. Microsoft, together with Yahoo, are capitalizing on this development.

> 'Today, search engines do a decent job of helping people navigate the Web and find information, but they don't do a very good job of enabling people to use the information they find,' said Steve Ballmer, Microsoft CEO. 'When we set out to build Bing, we grounded ourselves in a deep understanding of how people really want to use the Web.

> Bing is an important first step forward in our long-term effort to deliver innovations in search that enable people to find information quickly and use the information they've found to accomplish tasks and make smart decisions.'

Source: www.microsoft.com.

The Internet will develop further in the coming years as a buying medium, based on the behaviour of users. As a result, the buying process will be the focus when searching for information and, on the basis of the question asked (explicit question) the underlying need will also be analyzed (implicit questions). This leads to associations that make it easier and faster for the user to find sites and purchase online directly. Websites will be increasingly based on Internet anthropological knowledge: Why do users do what they do, and what do they really want? Additionally, the role played by emotion will become more and more important in this buying process and there will ultimately be an integration of physical experiences with virtual experiences at the individual level. In people's minds these experiences coalesce; a physical experience and a virtual experience are regarded as the same.[2]

Website builders will integrate this knowledge into the design of the site. There will be more emotion; fictional design using a combination of real images with fictional images, like the combination of drawings with real images and fictional images used in an animation. These creative possibilities are then an integration of the technological possibilities: film, webcam and photos that are integrated. Emotion and rationale then coalesce in the same way as physical and virtual (emotional) reality. Within the search process all these combinations of explicit and implicit questions have to be searched for more intensely. The Bing search engine is, in this context, a first step in that direction and the collaboration with Yahoo could be the basis for searching in terms of a buying process and the combination with Yahoo-based portals.

> *Microsoft Corp. today unveiled Bing, a new Decision Engine and consumer brand, providing customers with a first step in moving beyond search to help make faster, more informed decisions. Bing is specifically designed to build on the benefits of today's search engines but begins to move beyond this experience with a new approach to user experience and intuitive tools to help customers make better decisions, focusing initially on four key vertical areas: making a purchase decision, planning a trip, researching a health condition or finding a local shop or service.*
>
> *The result of this new approach is an important beginning for a new and more powerful kind of search service, which Microsoft is calling a Decision Engine, designed to empower people to gain insight and knowledge from the Web, moving more quickly to important decisions. The new service, located at http://www.Bing.com, will begin to roll out over the coming days and will be fully deployed worldwide on Wednesday, June 3.*

Source: www.microsoft.com.

---

2   In the book *Internet Overleven* [Surviving the Internet] (2007) I have described the four forms of reality: physical reality, imaginary reality (fantasy), mystical reality and binding reality. Everyone knows these forms and regard them as real because in one's mind they are experienced and felt to be real. On the Internet two of these forms – physical and emotional – are specifically relevant. In one's mind an experience on the Internet is felt and experienced as real. This also happens when reading a book for example, or watching a film.

The Internet is becoming an integral part of life in the western world. Each individual will use the Internet in their own way. In terms of shopping, the Internet will provide an infrastructure for physical shops that integrates the possibilities offered by web technology with the experience offered inside the physical store: customer recognition, buying suggestions and the creation of a particular ambience. For the web-shop, the Internet will be *the* channel. The possibilities will evolve quickly on the basis of the opportunities offered by the Internet. This will no longer be based on supporting existing processes, but will be an independent development which the unique Internet suppliers (endemic suppliers), in particular, must make maximum use of. But customers have to want to use the possibilities offered, it has to fit their way of life.

The Next Decade

When you are at home you can be yourself. The feeling of 'being at home' also means feeling affinity with the village or neighbourhood where you live; you need to feel comfortable there. Rather than just being a user of the Internet, where you feel you are a citizen of the world, you are also someone's neighbour. People will be living and spending more and more time in their own environment; the use of telecommunications means it's no longer necessary to always leave home to go shopping or to work. The home environment will therefore increase in significance.

In the 1980s the technique of socio-demographic characteristics was developed. This regarded neighbourhoods as clusters of like-minded people – people went to live where they felt comfortable. If this was not the case, for whatever reason, then these people would leave that neighbourhood, moving to places where they did feel happy with the people in the locality. Gradually neighbourhoods thus developed with like-minded people with uniform behaviour. Terms such as the 'gold coast neighbourhoods', the 'immigrant neighbourhoods', the 'problem neighbourhoods' and the 'student neighbourhoods' were used, to name but a few. The people defined the neighbourhood and attracted the facilities that were needed; the traders oriented themselves on the local residents. These definitions have not disappeared and will increasingly continue to define the character of a neighbourhood. Local shops will reappear but often as part of a joint venture or as a branch of a retail chain. The neighbourhood function and the local shops will steadily increase in importance precisely because more time will be spent in and around the home. Convenience goods will be offered by local shops whilst other items will be bought on the Internet or in large shopping centres.

The work function will also change. Working no longer means a 40-hour working week where partners leave each other in the morning to meet up again in the evening. More and more work-based tasks will be performed where they can be carried out most efficiently; use of existing infrastructures and the convergence of technologies means the need to be physically present in the organization will decrease. Work will increasingly come to the people instead of vice versa. The misconception sometimes arises that everyone could then always work from home; this is, however, incorrect. This will be a choice made by the individual and the organization based on the type of work to be performed.

The logic of doing work only in the office environment will disappear; often there will be a combination of working from home and in the office. This combination means that different demands will be made on how one lives; with a need for a defined work area and a consideration of the surroundings. Working from home can be a lonely experience and some enjoy the social interaction offered by a visit to their local shop in their break. This way of working will also influence the range of shops and the product range offered. Perhaps this will become more attractive and more sociable, for example, a coffee shop selling sandwiches. It is possible for local shops to capitalize on the needs of people who are at home more often and combine a home/work function. Shopping locally then becomes more than simply shopping for necessities, it becomes a social activity. The neighbourhoods will be convivial again, and perhaps the old 'village' feeling will return as well.

Another aspect that will also play a role in the regeneration of the local shop is the composition of the family. There will be a three-way split affecting the range of local shops:

- Double-income households without children: for these couples the local function is less significant, both partners work and if they work at home the local range of shops is less important; at best local shopping is carried out with a view to efficiency.

- Families with a care task, such as those with children: for these families the neighbourhood and local shops play an important role; convenience and social embedding are important elements. In this context the composition of the family is not as important as the care task and the children. That's also true of other care tasks that are relevant for this family. This may also include care for the ill or the elderly. In both cases there will be more instances of working from home, placing increased importance on the neighbourhood and local shops. The neighbourhood function is therefore very dependent on the home situation and how tied to the home one is. The range of shops and products offered will have to be harmonized to this, just like the atmosphere: efficiency or social embedding.

- Singles: a growing group that will increase to form approximately 33 per cent of the adult population. This group needs social contact. The home situation is not definitive for social behaviour and local shop behaviour. This group will in fact spend more time away from home, at work or partaking in social activities, hobbies or holidays. Shopping will be done wherever it suits. The attachment to the neighbourhood is limited for this group, with the exception of the elderly. For this particular group the neighbourhood is once again important because care is needed, mobility declines, and the social embedding in the neighbourhood is important for preventing loneliness. Shops will capitalize on this by organizing social activities and giving shopping an important social function. The coffee shops mentioned previously and little cafes are important.

People's behaviour in the future will naturally also be based on the commitments one has. It used to be normal, as an adult, to live with your family and to go to work outside the home. Often there was also a classic role pattern, in which one partner stayed at home, often the woman. In that scenario the local range of shops and the neighbourhood function was important. This has however been reduced by the increasing numbers of double-income and single-person households. Additionally, work and home functions have become separated, especially when mobility rapidly increased in the 1960s. This resulted in dormitory neighbourhoods and towns being created in which the social function was limited, likewise the range of shops. The attachment in these neighbourhoods was slight. In the future there will be a less rigid division between work and home, people are less dependent on the physical shops and the social climate in the neighbourhood or the village will become more and more important. Attachment to the home surroundings will increase strongly so that the local shops will once again have an important (social) function. These shops must harmonize their range on offer to the wishes of the local residents, which will make it possible for shopping to be fun again, and to regain a social function and the old village feeling.

Convergence

In Chapter 3 the development of technology in organizations is described. Fordism (up to 1960) moved into post-Fordism (up to 1990), during which computerization of existing processes became important. Computerization was initially 'process computerization' and this later became 'departmental computerization'. Work was performed by computers instead by people. There was a strong drive for efficiency without making any changes to the processes or ways of working. Around 1990 the pre-Internet era started, during which a communications infrastructure was established.

The start of the 1990s marked the era of the introduction of large infrastructures, such as the Internet and structures based on satellite and telecommunications (the mobile phone network). These infrastructures covered the world and were based on the behaviour or need of the individual. Suddenly new opportunities emerged. For instance, being able to call at any time, to any number and anywhere you wanted. Navigating on the basis of position recognition and street maps, watching your own TV stations wherever you were (even abroad) – it all became possible. People's behaviour was suddenly supported by technology. However, their behaviour didn't change substantially. With a mobile phone you were no longer tied to one place to make calls but this is still not a drastic change. The number of TV channels increased, but you still watched them at home, albeit on a flat screen with dozens of channels. The map on your lap has been replaced by an in-car GPS navigation system on the dashboard, but the behaviour is still the same. People still prefer to shop in stores that are familiar to them; despite the spectacular growth of the Internet as a buying medium it still only represents a small percentage of the total retail sales. But that will change.

Changes in People and Organizations

The recession of 2008 caused a break in the trend and organizations are now critically examining their own methods of functioning. The first response is to cut costs in order to maintain profitability. However, the new business model put an end to cost cutting; there will be a realization that perhaps the business model itself has to change. There will be a strong focus on the market and on the customer. This orientation will lead to a rethink of the company's own products and services on offer (focusing), of its own organization (flexibility and agility) and also of its business model. This reorientation is the foundation for an alternative use of the *resources* and the existing infrastructures. This is especially important because there is a sudden awareness amongst management that the business can't go on like this; a need for change arises.

The Internet user will also change; the behaviour will change through experience with the Internet, the intensity of use and the ease of access. Through changes in what's on offer – the addition of emotion and capitalizing on expected behaviour – and through the collaboration in terms of what's on offer (portals), a sort of cohesion will also occur on Internet, just as tribes came about in prehistoric times and how the large shopping centres formed. Searches on the Internet will change; search functionality will capitalize on the explicit and implicit wishes of the users. The infrastructures will converge, creating new opportunities. IT, Internet, satellites and telecommunications will offer facilities to organizations and people together as a single integrated infrastructure. This will bring about major changes in these organizations. The logic of going to work will disappear. Organizations will be much more loosely interconnected, based on the deployment of resources and the activities in the market. The infrastructures will be the binding factor, no longer the buildings or the personnel present. These organizations will be agile, able to adapt constantly to the changes in the market and in so doing to make use of the infrastructures to identify these changes. These organizations will exploit the changes to create a different organizational form, and to bind resources in a different manner, in terms of personnel, suppliers and customers.

As a consequence of this, the world of people will change. Choices can be made that fit the individual. This will lead to different forms of society and a different use of the infrastructure. Working and shopping will come to the people, who will integrate this into their living and home environment. Going out shopping and going out to work will become a personal choice for many people. There will, of course, still be limitations if there is a large physical component to a job role, such as house construction or working with machines in a factory. However, the virtual components, such as services, provision of services or creation, can be done in a different way. Communications can take place wherever, whenever and with whoever, and be very personal and very focused, by using the technological infrastructures. In the Internet era, which has actually only just started, people can be part of a world they choose and shape themselves. They will also be able to combine all of their tasks in a different way. Care tasks, shopping, working – everything converges on an individual basis. The new infrastructures facilitate this behaviour, but it's also down to the individual who has to want it. It remains a matter of choice!

Shopping 3.0

For physical shops, the Internet era will add a new dimension to the function of shopping, spanning place, time, distance and quantity.

Coffee is always on sale despite the fact that the harvest takes place only once a year and is sold in a quantity that people want – either a large or a small amount. The coffee is available to buy in the corner shop and you don't need to collect the beans from Brazil; commerce has made this possible.

This basic function of commerce has always existed and will always continue to exist. But the choice process of the customer is changing because of the possibilities offered by the new infrastructures. A new infrastructure is being created alongside physical shopping. Shopping via the Internet has advantages and disadvantages and web-shops will have to adapt on the basis of customer experiences and the different customer behaviour. The potential offered by technology will ensure that the virtual experience becomes more and more a physical experience, incorporating emotion along with the rational. Web-shops will integrate these technological possibilities so that there will be a 'buying experience' along with the rational needs of purchasing. The current disadvantages will be felt less and less by customers. The decision to shop online or in physical shops will become a personal and emotional choice. The Internet will come to occupy its own place with its own retailers and with customers who prefer to shop online. The customer will make a deliberate choice to either shop or to 'go to shops'. Stores will use more and more technology to make shopping more attractive and more emotional, but also to integrate rational aspects into the shop formula. Shops draw customers who have a strong preference for physical shopping; this may be because of the products (convenience goods), but also through personal motives, moment-defined motives or for social reasons.

In the coming decades there will be a big change in shopping. Shops will have to adapt to this in the same way as web retailers will have to. The Internet will initiate and facilitate an unprecedented change. Convergence will be the guiding message for shopping 3.0 behaviour in the technological, social and physical domains but ultimately it will be the customers who decide how, what and where they buy. The shops, whatever and wherever they are, can but get to know their customers and monitor them. The future of physical shops, but also of the web-shops, will be defined by taking advantage of 'shopping 3.0'. Happy customers are the aim of companies worldwide; technology enables this to happen on a large scale (see the letter from Nepal, Appendix 2). It will be an integrated world, with the Internet in stores and stores on the Internet; but the focus will be the customer, making you and me happy!

Appendix 1:
The Competing Values Model

Robert Quinn distinguished in organizations the so-called 'competing values': flexibility versus control and internally oriented versus externally oriented. This can be projected on market circumstances and leads to the following model (Figure A.1) (see also Chapter 3).

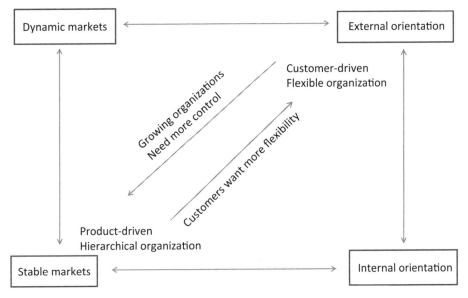

Figure A.1   The Competing Values model.
Source: Adapted from Quinn[1]

Four types of organization culture are the result of this, according to Quinn.

Organizations which are more internally orientated and are product driven are:

    1.   human relation-based: with a strong focus on cohesion;

1   Robert E. Quinn and John Rohrbauch, *Management Science*, Vol. 29, No. 3, March 1983.

2.   internal process relation-based: with a strong focus on processes.

Organizations which are more externally oriented and are customer driven are:

3.   open system relation-based: with a strong focus on growth and flexibility;

4.   goal-driven relation-based: with a strong focus on targets.

These types of organization each have their own culture and characteristics. In the retail sector, the consequences for customers are especially important. For the internally focused orientation, the process-based approach is important along with efficiency. With an external approach, flexibility is important in order to capitalize on changes. The consequences of a change of orientation are not only focused on the external expressions such as marketing and marketing communications, a modification in the culture is also important. On the Internet there are externally oriented organizations that constantly analyse their visitors and what they do on the site, and there are internally oriented organizations who offer a good range of products and services and fast delivery. For the latter, the service level agreement (SLA) is important while the externally oriented organizations regard customer contact and customer satisfaction as essential. Organizations that have been around for longer are considering an internally focused orientation to optimize the processes; they are aiming for control. With young organizations, it's the entrepreneurs who are flexible. The strain that exists between physical shops and online shops is often tension between the established organizations and the new young companies who capitalize on the new possibilities offered opportunistically.

Appendix 2

Swift Air Cargo Service P. Ltd.
P.O.Box: 2857
Kathmandu
Nepal

Tel: 977-1-4112152,4112294
977-1-4112238
Fax: 977-1-4112308

E-mail:tntktm@mos.com.np

www.tnt.com

July 9, 2010

A.R. Handicrafts
Lazimpat
Kathmandu, Nepal.

Kind Attention: Mr. Riyaz Khan.

Ref.: Special tariff for door to door courier service.

Dear Sir,

TNT International Express; a leading company in the name of international courier and cargo is serving over more than 200 countries and providing the best service having the international slogan *Sure we can*.

We are really grateful to gain your interest and faith upon our company, and hope for the eternal relationship between these two companies in the days ahead.

Referring to the subject, we enthusiastically propose our special offer to your esteemed organization. We believe it would be lucrative enough to meet your requirements.

Should you have any queries please feel free to contact us.

Ever happy to serve!

Thanks and regards,
Nishan Bhatta
Sales Executive
TNT express
TNT Complex, Airport Road
Tinkune, Kathmandu, Nepal

Tel: 977-1-4112152, 4112294, 4112238, 4112332
Fax: 977-1-4112308
Cell: 9849373845
Email: marketing@tntktm.wlink.com.np

Enclosed: Tariff for express document and parcel service.

Index

Figures are indicated by **bold** page numbers, tables by *italic* numbers.

A

adaptation for survival
  benefits of small organizations 84–7
  change as alternative to 77
  convergence of infrastructures 96–9
  demand driving supply 75–6
  economics as evolutionary 73–4
  entrepreneurship 75
  evaluation or evolution 76–7
  evolution 71–3
  exogenous/endogenous influences 78, 78–9
  flexibility and control 84–6
  historic perspective on change 87–94, *92*
  internal/external orientation 84–6
  Internet era 95–6
  need for focus on customers 79–81
  organizational changes 79–87
  problems with large companies 82–4
  social networking 81
  specialization 84
  transparency of the market 81
advertising
  and brands 20
  changes in 24

affiliate programmes 37–8
Amazon.co.uk 108
analysis software 154–6
appraisal of products by customers 29–30
architecture and the shop 3–4
augmented reality 181–2

B

barcodes 140–1
Barnes & Noble 110
barriers to cross-border trading 68–70
behaviour, customer
  analysis of 154–6, 161–2
  changes in 12–14, **14**
  convenience/shopping/luxury 176–8, *178*
  cross-border buying 63–5
  and gender 58
  information searches 39
  information/buying behaviour split 190
  Internet's impact on 30, *31*
  physical/online *40*
  preferences and routines 186
  range of goods available 17
  rational/emotional 16–17, 46–9
  shops lack of response to changes 31
  support through recommendations 179

see also customers; recognition of
     customers
Benschop, Albert 189
Best Buy 101–2
Bijenkorf department store 50
Bing 131–2, 133–4, 188, 191
biometric fingerprint payment 124
Blue Tomato 168
body scanning 125
book trade
     audio books 114
     changes in 108–10
     e-books and e-readers 114–17, 180
     impact of Internet 113, 114–17
Borders 109–10
Bose 123
brands 19–22
     appraisal of products 29–30
     belonging, feeling of 29–30
     non-food 29–30
     preference for 47
     product brands v. own brands
          26–8
business intelligence 154–6
business models, need for new
     179–80
Business Objects 156
buying
     as focus for information searching
          190
     reasons for 42–3
buying behaviour
     changes in 12–14, **14**
     costs/prices 127–9
     cross-border buying 63–5
     functional 52–3
     and gender 58, 66–7
     information searches 39
     Internet's impact on 30, *31*
     physical/online *40*
     range of goods available 17

rational/emotional 16–17, 46–9
     shops lack of response to changes
          31
     split with information searching
          190
     of women 66–7
buying moment, focus on 111
buying process 2, 185–92, **186**

C
call centres 24
change
     historic perspective on 87–94, *92*
     in online buying process 185–92,
          186
     in people and organizations
          195–7
     in society 5–6
changing rooms 125–6, 181–2
Chief Financial Officers (CFOs) 93
collaboration
     between companies 91, 130–1,
          187–8
     in product development 125
communication
     with customers 33
     focused 25–6
     increased levels of 91
comparison websites 41–2, 131
compensation for web price
          differences 60
competing values model 84, 85, **85**,
          85n12, **199**, 199–200
computerization *see* technology
confidence in online retailers 61–2
consignation 141
consumptionism 88, 89
convenience goods 55, 181–2
convenience of online shopping 32
convergence of infrastructures 96–9
costs for shops/webshops 127–9

credit crisis of 2008 91
cross-border trading 63–5, 68–70
cross-channel approach 156–61, **161,**
    163–6, **164,** *165*
cross-channel business model 98, 99,
    127, 156–61
cultural differences in cross-border
    buying 64–5
customer relationship marketing
    151–4, **153**
customer value 21–2, 23
customers
    analysis of behaviour 154–6
    appraisal of products by 29–30
    buying process of 2
    as central on the Internet 2–3
    changes in buying behaviour
        12–14, **14**
    changing needs of 1–2
    collaboration in product
        development 125
    communication with 33–4
    decision-making by 58
    direct sales to 28, **29**
    group buying 125
    historic development of *92*
    influences on **18**
    information of in RFID chips 143
    information searches by 39, 57–8,
        61
    knowledge, possession of by 59
    knowledge of 16
    loyalty of 23, 49–50
    need for focus on 79–81
    obtaining information on 25–6
    personal motives 35
    price and buying motives 48–9
    profiles of 152–4, **153,** 179
    recognition of by shops 13
    reviews by 57
    in shopping 3.0 model 57–60

social networking of 81
    see also behaviour, customer;
        recognition of customers

D
Darwin, Charles 71–3
decision-making by customers 58
demand
    as driving supply 75–6
    era driven by 25–6, **26**
    individualization of 25
    need for focus on customers
        79–81
design of websites 191
Diako Easyfit 150–1, 162
digicities 130–1
digital natives 15, **15,** 101
digitization 117–19, **118, 119,** 121–7,
    124
direct marketing 24–5
direct sales to customers 28, **29**
distribution channel
    book trade 108–10
    digitization 117–19, **118, 119**
    first phase of changes in 120–1
    by specialized companies 146
dual pricing strategy 36

E
ease of online shopping 32
e-books 114–17, 180
e-commerce
    first phase of changes 120–1
    impact of future rise on 38, **38**
    second phase of changes 121–7,
        124
    see also online shopping
economics as evolutionary 73–4
education and digital natives 101
efficiency in shopping 52
emotional behaviour 17, 46–9

integration with rational 191
loyalty based on 49–50
endemic business model 98–9, 109,
   109n1
endogenous/exogenous influences
   78, 78–9
enjoyment element of shopping 53–4
entrepreneurship 75
   flexibility and control 86
   and the Internet 95–6
e-readers 114–17
e-tailing, impact of future rise on 38,
   38
   see also online shopping
European Union (EU) 68–70
evaluation or evolution 76–7
evolution of shopping
   benefits of small organizations
      84–7
   change as alternative to
      adaptation 77
   convergence of infrastructures
      96–9
   demand driving supply 75–6
   economics as evolutionary 73–4
   entrepreneurship 75
   evaluation or evolution 76–7
   exogenous/endogenous influences
      78, 78–9
   flexibility and control 84–6
   historic perspective on change
      87–94, 92
   internal/external orientation 84–6
   Internet era 95–6
   need for focus on customers
      79–81
   organizational changes 79–87
   problems with large companies
      82–4
   social networking 81
   specialization 84

theory of evolution 72–3
transparency of the market 81
exclusiveness as reason for buying
   43
exogenous/endogenous influences
   78, 78–9
experiences
   integration of physical and virtual
      190–1
   marketing 35
   shopping 54–6
external/internal orientation 84–6

F
families
   composition of 193–4
   as reason for buying 43
Fashionista virtual dressing room
   181–2
fingerprint payment 124
flexibility and control 84–6
food sector
   rational purchases 46
   routine, role of 46
Fordism 87–8, 100
functional shopping 52–3

G
Galapagos Islands 71–2
gender and buying behaviour 58,
   66–7
Germany 94
gifts as reason for buying 43
Google 129–30, 132, 188
grocery sector
   and brands 20–1
   price wars 49
group buying 125

H
haggling 55, 56

Harrods 54
hedonistic shopping 53–6
High Streets, difficulties faced by
11–12
historic perspective on change 87–94,
92
holiday shopping 55, 56
holograms, sales assistants as 126
home deliveries 52, 167–8
home environment, importance of
192–3, 194–5
home pages, personalized 185–7, **186**
homeworking 193
Hybris software 163–6, **164,** *165*

I
IBM 155
IKEA 34–5
imitation as reason for buying 43
impulse buying 55
individualization of demand 25
Industrial Revolution 87
information
    and buying, behaviour split 190
    customer, in RFID chips 143
    on products, searches for 39,
        57–8, 61, 129–32
infrastructures, convergence of 96–9
Inquiry into the Nature and Cause of the
        Wealth of Nations, An (Smith) 74
internal/external orientation 84–6
Internet
    buying behaviour *40*
    challenges introduced by 18–19
    changes in the future 185–92
    changes in users 196
    communication with customers
        33–4
    convenience of 32
    customer relationship marketing
        151–4, **153**

customers as central 2–3
ease of shopping on 32
entrepreneurial phase 95–6
era of 95–6, 100
first phase of changes due to
        120–1
immigrants and natives 15, **15**
impact of 97, **107,** 107–10, 113–17
impact of future rise in shopping
        on 38, **38**
impact on buying behaviour 31,
        31
increase in usage 36
information/buying behaviour
        split 190
integration into shops 183
integration with 145–7, **147**
new phase of 188–9
period prior to 90–1, 95, 100
reasons for shopping on 32–4
second phase of changes due to
        121–7, **124**
shopping malls on 37–8, 130–1
shops selling via 37–9
statistics on use 132–3
as threat to shops 36
user behaviour 189
invisible hand theory 74, 75

J
John Lewis 112–13, 149–50

K
knowledge, customers' possession
        of 59
Kuneva, Meglena 68

L
large companies, problems with 82–4
leisure activity, shopping as 34–5,
        42–3

local shops 176, 192, 193, 194–5
logistics services 146
loyalty of customers 23, 49–50
luxury items, technology for 184–5

M
Madoff, Bernard Lawrence 'Bernie'
    93n13
management
    in large organizations 82–4
    by spreadsheets 82n8
    transformation of 86
manufacturers
    direct sales to customers 28, **29**
    imbalance in relationship with
        shops 27–8
    relationship with retailers 123,
        141
marketing, experience 35
mass production and consumption
    87–8
media, power of 90
Mediamarkt 35
men, shopping behaviour of 52–3
Microsoft 131–4, 155–6
migration 90–1
mobile phones
    RFID chips in 142
    shopping by 126
monotony of town centres 11–12
motives of customers 35
multi channel approach 148–51
music retail
    digitization 117–19, **118, 119**
    impact of Internet 113–14

N
narrowcasting 143–5
natural selection, theory of 72–3
near field communications (NFC)
    142–3, 183–4

neighbourhoods, importance of
    192–3, 194
Netherlands 94
networked shopping 125
new retailing 134, **135**
newspapers as e-books 116
Nike 158

O
Octopus cards 161–2
online retailers
    confidence in 61–2
    purchasing channels 36
    real shops use of 37–9
online shopping
    advantages/disadvantages 41
    buying behaviour 40
    changes in the future 185–92, **186**
    as a choice 197
    communication with customers
        33–4
    convenience of 32
    differences to real 40
    ease of 32
    and emotional shopping needs 67
    impact of future rise in 38, **38**
    impact on buying behaviour 31, *31*
    motives for 32–4
    routine 63–4
online support, retailers' use of 111
opening hours, restrictions on 9–10
optimization of sales points 110–11
ORCA buying model **14**
organizations
    changes in 195–6
    structure of 86
orientation of companies, internal/
    external 84–6
Origin of Species, The (Darwin) 73
out of town centres, development of
    4–5

own brands v. product brands 26–8
Oyster cards 161–2

P
personal motives of customers 35
personalized home pages 185–7,
        186
physical needs, satisfaction of 42
physical products, split with virtual
        products 122–3, 124
physical shopping
    advantages/disadvantages 41
    differences to online *40*
pick up places 121
portals 133–4
post-Fordism 89–90
prices
    and buying motives 48–9
    comparison 13–14
    for shops/webshops 127–9
    strategy 36
private-label brands v. product
        brands 26–8
product brands v. own brands 26–8
products
    categories of 17
    information searches for 39
    range of goods available 17
    technological recognition of 140–5
profiles of customers 152–4, **153,** 179
purchasing channels 36

Q
Quinn, Robert 84, 85, 199

R
radio frequency identification (RFID)
        chips 111, 141–5, 181–4
range of goods available 17, 22
rational behaviour 16–17, 46–9, 52,
        191

real shopping
    advantages/disadvantages 41
    as a choice 197
    differences to online *40*
    difficulties faced by 11
reality, four forms of 191n2
reasons for buying 42–3
recognition of customers 13
    buying moment, focus on 111
    cross-channel approach 156–61,
        161
    digitization 117–19, **118, 119**
    in the future 185–6
    impact of the Internet **107,** 107–17
    importance of 105
    narrowcastng 144–5
    online support, retailers' use of
        111
    optimization of sales points
        110–11
    specialised/general stores 112–13
recognizability of brands 19–20
recreation, shopping as 34–5, 42–3
relationship building 25–6, 40
retail
    development of *92*
    new developments 124–6
    new retailing 134, **135**
    restructuring of 123–4
retailers
    buying moment, focus on 111
    challenges faced by 18–19
    compensation for web price
        differences 60
    cross-channel approach by
        156–61, **161**
    difficult times for 1–2, 10–12
    extra effort from 60–1
    first phase of changes 120–1
    future of 102–4
    impact of Internet on **107,** 107–10

knowledge of customers,
    importance of 16
lack of response to changes in
    buying behaviour 31
obtaining information on
    customers 25–6
online support, use of by 111
optimization of sales points
    110–11
outside capital, result of using
    94
relationship building 40
relationship with manufacturers/
    suppliers 123, 141
RFID technology 111, 141–5,
    181–4
second phase of changes 121–7,
    124
selling via the Internet 37–9
specialised/general stores 112–13
transaction-oriented approach
    45–6
webcams, use of by 62–3
websites for 134
reviews by customers 57
RFID technology 111, 141–5, 181–4
routine
    customers' preference for 186
    online shopping 63–4
    role of in buying behaviour 50
    role of in buying food 46

S
sales points, optimization of 110–11
SAP 156
satisfaction of physical needs 42
scarcity 74n3
Scholl 170–2
search process 129–32
Selexyz 38, 145
Selfridges 135–6

shopping
    development of 173–5
    enjoyment element of 53–4
    as fun and relaxing 4
    functional 52–3
    hedonistic 53–6
    as leisure activity 34–5, 42–3,
        176–7
    reasons for 42–3
shopping 3.0 model **56,** 57–60, *59*
shopping goods, technology for
    182–4
shopping malls on the Internet 37–8
shopping/convenience goods 55
shops
    challenges faced by 18–19
    compensation for web
        price differences 60
    development of 4–5, **5**
    extra effort from 60–1
    growth in types of *12*
    imbalance in relationship
        with suppliers 27–8
    influences on **18**
    Internet as threat to 36
    lack of response to changes
        in buying behaviour 31
    loyalty to 23
    obtaining information on
        customers 25–6
    opening hours, restrictions
        on 9–10
    selling via the Internet 37–9
    webcams, use of by 62–3
shops, architecture and design of 3–4
small organizations, benefits of 84–7
small shops
    loyalty to 23
    move towards 87
smart carts 125, 181
Smith, Adam 71, 73, 74, 87

sociable shoppers 53–4
social loyalty 49–50
social networking 57, 81, 126
society, changes in 5–6
specialization 84, 146
spreadsheet management 82n8
stakeholders, focus on since 1990s 93
Starbucks 34
stock control 141
structural loyalty 50
structure of organizations 86
suppliers
    collaboration between 130–1,
        187–8
    demand as driving 75–6
    direct sales to customers 28, **29**
    imbalance in relationship with
        shops 27–8
    relationship with retailers 123,
        141
supply economy 82, 82n7
SWOT analysis 78

T
technology
    and advertising 24–5
    barcodes 140–1
    Blue Tomato 168
    case studies 168–72
    convenience goods 181–2
    convenience/shopping/luxury
        goods 177–8, *178*
    for cross-channel approach 163–6,
        164, *165*
    customer analysis 154–6
    customer relationship marketing
        151–4, **153**
    development of *92*
    impact of 5–6
    integration with the Internet
        145–7, **147**

luxury items 184–5
multi channel approach 148–51
narrowcasting 143–5
near field communications (NFC)
        183–4
    need for and aims of in retail
        139–40
    radio frequency identification
        (RFID) chips 141–5, 181–4
    recognition at product level 140–5
    shopping goods 182–4
    Waterstones **169,** 169–70
telemarketing 24
Tesco 49
town centres
    development of 4–5
    difficulties faced by 11–12
Tracy, M. 99
trading sites 130
transaction-oriented approach of
        retailers 45–6
transparency of the market 81
trolleys, shopping 125, 181
trust in online shopping 63–4

V
value, customer 21–2, 23
vendor managed inventory (VMI)
        141
Victoria's Secret 159–60
virtual products, split with physical
        products 122–3, 124

W
Walmart 49
Waterstones **169,** 169–70
Wealth of Nations (Smith) 74
web browsers 132, *133*
web retailers
    confidence in 61–2
    customers as central 2–3

disadvantages of 3
purchasing channels 36
real shops use of 37–9
web shopping
    advantages/disadvantages 41
    buying behaviour 40
    changes in the future 185–92, 1
        86
    as a choice 197
    communication with customers
        33–4
    convenience of 32
    differences to real 40
    ease of 32
    and emotional shopping needs
        67
    impact of future rise in 38, 38

impact on buying behaviour 30,
    31
motives for 32–4
routine 63–4
webcams 62–3
websites
    comparison 41–2
    popular in UK 35
    and routine 63–4
WH Smith 110
Wiersema, F. 99
women and buying behaviour 66–7
Woolworths 50–1
work, location of 193, 196

Y
Yahoo! 155–6